Autonomous Vehicle Driverless Self-Driving Cars and Artificial Intelligence

Practical Advances in Artificial Intelligence (AI) and Machine Learning

Dr. Lance Eliot

and

Michael B. Eliot

Disclaimer: This book is presented solely for educational and entertainment purposes. The author and publisher are not offering it as legal, accounting, or other professional services advice. The author and publisher make no representations or warranties of any kind and assume no liabilities of any kind with respect to the accuracy or completeness of the contents and specifically disclaim any implied warranties of merchantability or fitness of use for a particular purpose. Neither the author nor the publisher shall be held liable or responsible to any person or entity with respect to any loss or incidental or consequential damages caused, or alleged to have been caused, directly or indirectly, by the information or programs contained herein. Every company is different and the advice and strategies contained herein may not be suitable for your situation.

ISBN: 0692051023
ISBN-13: 978-0692051023

DEDICATION

To my incredible daughter, Lauren, and my incredible son, Michael.

Forest fortuna adiuvat (from the Latin; good fortune favors the brave).

CONTENTS

ACKNOWLEDGMENTS

I have been the beneficiary of advice and counsel by many friends, colleagues, family, investors, and many others. I want to thank everyone that has aided me throughout my career. I write from the heart and the head, having experienced first-hand what it means to have others around you that support you during the good times and the tough times.

To Warren Bennis, one of my doctoral advisors and ultimately a colleague, I offer my deepest thanks and appreciation, especially for his calm and insightful wisdom and support.

To Mark Stevens and his generous efforts toward funding and supporting the USC Stevens Center for Innovation.

To Lloyd Greif and the USC Lloyd Greif Center for Entrepreneurial Studies for their ongoing encouragement of founders and entrepreneurs.

To Peter Drucker, William Wang, Aaron Levie, Peter Kim, Jon Kraft, Cindy Crawford, Jenny Ming, Steve Milligan, Chis Underwood, Frank Gehry, Buzz Aldrin, Steve Forbes, Bill Thompson, Dave Dillon, Alan Fuerstman, Larry Ellison, Jim Sinegal, John Sperling, Mark Stevenson, Anand Nallathambi, Thomas Barrack, Jr., and many other innovators and leaders that I have met and gained mightily from doing so.

Thanks to Ed Trainor, Kevin Anderson, James Hickey, Wendell Jones, Ken Harris, DuWayne Peterson, Mike Brown, Jim Thornton, Abhi Beniwal, Al Biland, John Nomura, Eliot Weinman, John Desmond, and many others for their unwavering support during my career.

And most of all thanks as always to Lauren and Michael, for their ongoing support and for having seen me writing and heard much of this material during the many months involved in writing it. To their patience and willingness to listen.

Dr. Lance Eliot and Michael B. Eliot

INTRODUCTION BY LANCE ELIOT

This is a book that provides the newest innovations and the latest Artificial Intelligence (AI) advances about the emerging nature of AI-based autonomous self-driving driverless cars. My son, Michael Eliot, provided key research, review, input, and insights for this book, and also was the sole author for the last chapter, and thus he's listed as a co-author for the book – I am indebted to him for his efforts on this endeavor. Our respective bios are included toward the end of the book in the section entitled "About the Authors."

Via recent advances in Artificial Intelligence (AI) and Machine Learning (ML), we are nearing the day when vehicles can control themselves and will not require and nor rely upon human intervention to perform their driving tasks (or, that <u>allow</u> for human intervention, but only *require* human intervention in very limited ways).

Similar to my other related books, which I describe in a moment and list the chapters in the Appendix A of this book, I am particularly focused on those advances that pertain to self-driving cars. The phrase "autonomous vehicles" is often used to refer to any kind of vehicle, whether it is ground-based or in the air or sea, and whether it is a cargo hauling trailer truck or a conventional passenger car. Though the aspects described in this book are certainly applicable to all kinds of autonomous vehicles, I am focused more so here on cars.

Indeed, I am especially known for my role in aiding the advancement of self-driving cars, serving currently as the Executive Director of the Cybernetic Self-Driving Cars Institute.. In addition to writing software, designing and developing systems and software for self-driving cars, I also speak and write quite a bit about the topic. This book is a collection of some of my more advanced essays. For those of you that might have seen my essays posted elsewhere, I have updated them and integrated them into this book as one handy cohesive package.

You might be interested in companion books that I have written that cover additional key innovations and fundamentals about self-driving cars.

Those books are entitled "**Advances in AI and Autonomous Vehicles: Cybernetic Self-Driving Cars**," "**Self-Driving Cars: "The Mother of All AI Projects**," "**Innovation and Thought Leadership on Self-Driving Driverless Cars**," and "**New Advances in AI Autonomous Driverless Self-Driving Cars**" (they are all available via Amazon). See Appendix A of this herein book to see a listing of the chapters covered in those three books.

For the introduction here to this book, I am going to borrow my introduction from those companion books, since it does a good job of laying out the landscape of self-driving cars and my overall viewpoints on the topic. And, the first chapter is my overall framework for AI self-driving cars that I have used throughout my efforts as a guiding compass. The remainder of the book is all new material that does not appear in any of the companion books.

INTRODUCTION TO SELF-DRIVING CARS

This is a book about self-driving cars. Someday in the future, we'll all have self-driving cars and this book will perhaps seem antiquated, but right now, we are at the forefront of the self-driving car wave. Daily news bombards us with flashes of new announcements by one car maker or another and leaves the impression that within the next few weeks or maybe months that the self-driving car will be here. A casual non-technical reader would assume from these news flashes that in fact we must be on the cusp of a true self-driving car.

Here's a real news flash: We are still quite a distance from having a true self-driving car. It is years to go before we get there.

Why is that? Because a true self-driving car is akin to a moonshot. In the same manner that getting us to the moon was an incredible feat, likewise can it be said for achieving a true self-driving car. Anybody that suggests or even brashly states that the true self-driving car is nearly here should be viewed with great skepticism. Indeed, you'll see that I often tend to use the word "hogwash" or "crock" when I assess much of the decidedly *fake news* about self-driving cars. Those of us on the inside know that what is often reported to the outside is malarkey. Few of the insiders are willing to say so. I have no such hesitation.

Indeed, I've been writing a popular blog post about self-driving cars and hitting hard on those that try to wave their hands and pretend that we are on the imminent verge of true self-driving cars. For many years, I've been known as the AI Insider. Besides writing about AI, I also develop AI software. I do what I describe. It also gives me insights into what others that are doing AI are really doing versus what it is said they are doing.

Many faithful readers had asked me to pull together my insightful short essays and put them into another book, which you are now holding in your hands.

For those of you that have been reading my essays over the years, this collection not only puts them together into one handy package, I also updated the essays and added new material. For those of you that are new to the topic of self-driving cars and AI, I hope you find these essays approachable and informative. I also tend to have a writing style with a bit of a voice, and so you'll see that I am times have a wry sense of humor and also like to poke at conformity.

As a former professor and founder of an AI research lab, I for many years wrote in the formal language of academic writing. I published in referred journals and served as an editor for several AI journals. This writing here is not of the nature, and I have adopted a different and more informal style for these essays. That being said, I also do mention from time-to-time more rigorous material on AI and encourage you all to dig into those deeper and more formal materials if so interested.

I am also an AI practitioner. This means that I write AI software for a living. Currently, I head-up the Cybernetics Self-Driving Car Institute, where we are developing AI software for self-driving cars. I am excited to also report that my son, also a software engineer, heads-up our Cybernetics Self-Driving Car Lab. What I have helped to start, and for which he is an integral part, ultimately he will carry long into the future after I have retired. My daughter, a marketing whiz, also is integral to our efforts as head of our Marketing group. She too will carry forward the legacy now being formulated.

For those of you that are reading this book and have a penchant for writing code, you might consider taking a look at the open source code available for self-driving cars. This is a handy place to start learning how to develop AI for self-driving cars. There are also many new educational courses spring forth.

There is a growing body of those wanting to learn about and develop self-driving cars, and a growing body of colleges, labs, and other avenues by which you can learn about self-driving cars.

This book will provide a foundation of aspects that I think will get you ready for those kinds of more advanced training opportunities. If you've already taken those classes, you'll likely find these essays especially interesting as they offer a perspective that I am betting few other instructors or faculty offered to you. These are challenging essays that ask you to think beyond the conventional about self-driving cars.

THE MOTHER OF ALL AI PROJECTS

In June 2017, Apple CEO Tim Cook came out and finally admitted that Apple has been working on a self-driving car. As you'll see in my essays, Apple was enmeshed in secrecy about their self-driving car efforts. We have only been able to read the tea leaves and guess at what Apple has been up to. The notion of an iCar has been floating for quite a while, and self-driving engineers and researchers have been signing tight-lipped Non-Disclosure Agreements (NDA's) to work on projects at Apple that were as shrouded in mystery as any military invasion plans might be.

Tim Cook said something that many others in the Artificial Intelligence (AI) field have been saying, namely, the creation of a self-driving car has got to be the mother of all AI projects. In other words, it is in fact a tremendous moonshot for AI. If a self-driving car can be crafted and the AI works as we hope, it means that we have made incredible strides with AI and that therefore it opens many other worlds of potential breakthrough accomplishments that AI can solve.

Is this hyperbole? Am I just trying to make AI seem like a miracle worker and so provide self-aggrandizing statements for those of us writing the AI software for self-driving cars? No, it is not hyperbole. Developing a true self-driving car is really, really, really hard to do. Let me take a moment to explain why. As a side note, I realize that the Apple CEO is known for at times uttering hyperbole, and he had previously said for example that the year 2012 was "the mother of all years," and he had said that the release of iOS 10 was "the mother of all releases" – all of which does suggest he likes to use the handy "mother of" expression. But, I assure you, in terms of true self-driving cars, he has hit the nail on the head. For sure.

When you think about a moonshot and how we got to the moon, there are some identifiable characteristics and those same aspects can be applied to creating a true self-driving car. You'll notice that I keep putting the word "true" in front of the self-driving car expression. I do so because as per my essay about the various levels of self-driving cars (see Chapter 3), there are some self-driving cars that are only somewhat of a self-driving car. The somewhat versions are ones that require a human driver to be ready to intervene. In my view, that's not a true self-driving car. A true self-driving car is one that requires no human driver intervention at all. It is a car that can entirely undertake via automation the driving task without any human driver needed. This is the essence of what is known as a Level 5 self-driving car. We are currently at the Level 2 and Level 3 mark, and not yet at Level 5.

Getting to the moon involved aspects such as having big stretch goals, incremental progress, experimentation, innovation, and so on. Let's review how this applied to the moonshot of the bygone era, and how it applies to the self-driving car moonshot of today.

Big Stretch Goal

Trying to take a human and deliver the human to the moon, and bring them back, safely, was an extremely large stretch goal at the time. No one knew whether it could be done. The technology wasn't available yet. The cost was huge. The determination would need to be fierce. Etc. To reach a Level 5 self-driving car is going to be the same. It is a big stretch goal. We can readily get to the Level 3, and we are able to see the Level 4 just up ahead, but a Level 5 is still an unknown as to if it is doable. It should eventually be doable and in the same way that we thought we'd eventually get to the moon, but when it will occur is a different story.

Incremental Progress

Getting to the moon did not happen overnight in one fell swoop. It took years and years of incremental progress to get there. Likewise for self-driving cars. Google has famously been striving to get to the Level 5, and pretty much been willing to forgo dealing with the intervening levels, but most of the other self-driving car makers are doing the incremental route. Let's get a good Level 2 and a somewhat Level 3 going. Then, let's improve the Level 3 and get a somewhat Level 4 going. Then, let's improve the Level 4 and finally arrive at a Level 5. This seems to be the prevalent way that we are going to achieve the true self-driving car.

Experimentation

You likely know that there were various experiments involved in perfecting the approach and technology to get to the moon. As per making incremental progress, we first tried to see if we could get a rocket to go into space and safety return, then put a monkey in there, then with a human, then we went all the way to the moon but didn't land, and finally we arrived at the mission that actually landed on the moon. Self-driving cars are the same way. We are doing simulations of self-driving cars. We do testing of self-driving cars on private land under controlled situations. We do testing of self-driving cars on public roadways, often having to meet regulatory requirements including for example having an engineer or equivalent in the car to take over the controls if needed. And so on. Experiments big and small are needed to figure out what works and what doesn't.

Innovation

There are already some advances in AI that are allowing us to progress toward self-driving cars. We are going to need even more advances. Innovation in all aspects of technology are going to be required to achieve a true self-driving car. By no means do we already have everything in-hand that we need to get there. Expect new inventions and new approaches, new algorithms, etc.

Setbacks

Most of the pundits are avoiding talking about potential setbacks in the progress toward self-driving cars. Getting to the moon involved many setbacks, some of which you never have heard of and were buried at the time so as to not dampen enthusiasm and funding for getting to the moon. A recurring theme in many of my included essays is that there are going to be setbacks as we try to arrive at a true self-driving car. Take a deep breath and be ready. I just hope the setbacks don't completely stop progress. I am sure that it will cause progress to alter in a manner that we've not yet seen in the self-driving car field. I liken the self-driving car of today to the excitement everyone had for Uber when it first got going. Today, we have a different view of Uber and with each passing day there are more regulations to the ride sharing business and more concerns raised. The darling child only stays a darling until finally that child acts up. It will happen the same with self-driving cars.

SELF-DRIVING CARS CHALLENGES

But what exactly makes things so hard to have a true self-driving car, you might be asking. You have seen cruise control for years and years. You've lately seen cars that can do parallel parking. You've seen YouTube videos of Tesla drivers that put their hands out the window as their car zooms along the highway, and seen to therefore be in a self-driving car. Aren't we just needing to put a few more sensors onto a car and then we'll have in-hand a true self-driving car? Nope.

Consider for a moment the nature of the driving task. We don't just let anyone at any age drive a car. Worldwide, most countries won't license a driver until the age of 18, though many do allow a learner's permit at the age of 15 or 16. Some suggest that a younger age would be physically too small to reach the controls of the car. Though this might be the case, we could easily adjust the controls to allow for younger aged and thus smaller stature. It's not their physical size that matters. It's their cognitive development that matters.

To drive a car, you need to be able to reason about the car, what the car can and cannot do. You need to know how to operate the car. You need to know about how other cars on the road drive. You need to know what is allowed in driving such as speed limits and driving within marked lanes. You need to be able to react to situations and be able to avoid getting into accidents. You need to ascertain when to hit your brakes, when to steer clear of a pedestrian, and how to keep from ramming that motorcyclist that just cut you off.

Many of us had taken courses on driving. We studied about driving and took driver training. We had to take a test and pass it to be able to drive. The point being that though most adults take the driving task for granted, and we often "mindlessly" drive our cars, there is a significant amount of cognitive effort that goes into driving a car. After a while, it becomes second nature. You don't especially think about how you drive, you just do it. But, if you watch a novice driver, say a teenager learning to drive, you suddenly realize that there is a lot more complexity to it than we seem to realize.

Furthermore, driving is a very serious task. I recall when my daughter and son first learned to drive. They are both very conscientious people. They wanted to make sure that whatever they did, they did well, and that they did not harm anyone. Every day, when you get into a car, it is probably around 4,000 pounds of hefty metal and plastics (about two tons), and it is a lethal weapon. Think about it. You drive down the street in an object that weighs two tons and with the engine it can accelerate and ram into anything you want to hit. The damage a car can inflict is very scary. Both my children were surprised that they were being given the right to maneuver this monster of a beast that could cause tremendous harm entirely by merely letting go of the steering wheel for a moment or taking your eyes off the road.

In fact, in the United States alone there are about 30,000 deaths per year by auto accidents, which is around 100 per day. Given that there are about 263 million cars in the United States, I am actually more amazed that the number of fatalities is not a lot higher. During my morning commute, I look at all the thousands of cars on the freeway around me, and I think that if all of them decided to go zombie and drive in a crazy maniac way, there would be many people dead. Somehow, incredibly, each day, most people drive relatively safely. To me, that's a miracle right there. Getting millions and millions of people to be safe and sane when behind the wheel of a two ton mobile object, it's a feat that we as a society should admire with pride.

So, hopefully you are in agreement that the driving task requires a great deal of cognition. You don't' need to be especially smart to drive a car, and we've done quite a bit to make car driving viable for even the average dolt. There isn't an IQ test that you need to take to drive a car. If you can read and write, and pass a test, you pretty much can legally drive a car. There are of course some that drive a car and are not legally permitted to do so, plus there are private areas such as farms where drivers are young, but for public roadways in the United States, you can be generally of average intelligence (or less) and be able to legally drive.

This though makes it seem like the cognitive effort must not be much. If the cognitive effort was truly hard, wouldn't we only have Einstein's that could drive a car? We have made sure to keep the driving task as simple as we can, by making the controls easy and relatively standardized, and by having roads that are relatively standardized, and so on. It is as though Disneyland has put their Autopia into the real-world, by us all as a society agreeing that roads will be a certain way, and we'll all abide by the various rules of driving.

A modest cognitive task by a human is still something that stymies AI. You certainly know that AI has been able to beat chess players and be good at other kinds of games. This type of narrow cognition is not what car driving is about. Car driving is much wider. It requires knowledge about the world, which a chess playing AI system does not need to know. The cognitive aspects of driving are on the one hand seemingly simple, but at the same time require layer upon layer of knowledge about cars, people, roads, rules, and a myriad of other "common sense" aspects. We don't have any AI systems today that have that same kind of breadth and depth of awareness and knowledge.

As revealed in my essays, the self-driving car of today is using trickery to do particular tasks. It is all very narrow in operation. Plus, it currently assumes that a human driver is ready to intervene. It is like a child that we have taught to stack blocks, but we are needed to be right there in case the child stacks them too high and they begin to fall over. AI of today is brittle, it is narrow, and it does not approach the cognitive abilities of humans. This is why the true self-driving car is somewhere out in the future.

Another aspect to the driving task is that it is not solely a mind exercise. You do need to use your senses to drive. You use your eyes a vision sensors to see the road ahead. You vision capability is like a streaming video, which your brain needs to continually analyze as you drive. Where is the road? Is there a pedestrian in the way? Is there another car ahead of you? Your senses are relying a flood of info to your brain. Self-driving cars are trying to do the same, by using cameras, radar, ultrasound, and lasers. This is an attempt at mimicking how humans have senses and sensory apparatus.

Thus, the driving task is mental and physical. You use your senses, you use your arms and legs to manipulate the controls of the car, and you use your brain to assess the sensory info and direct your limbs to act upon the controls of the car. This all happens instantly. If you've ever perhaps gotten something in your eye and only had one eye available to drive with, you suddenly realize how dependent upon vision you are. If you have a broken foot with a cast, you suddenly realize how hard it is to control the brake pedal and the accelerator. If you've taken medication and your brain is maybe sluggish, you suddenly realize how much mental strain is required to drive a car.

An AI system that plays chess only needs to be focused on playing chess. The physical aspects aren't important because usually a human moves the chess pieces or the chessboard is shown on an electronic display. Using AI for a more life-and-death task such as analyzing MRI images of patients, this again does not require physical capabilities and instead is done by examining images of bits.

Driving a car is a true life-and-death task. It is a use of AI that can easily and at any moment produce death. For those colleagues of mine that are developing this AI, as am I, we need to keep in mind the somber aspects of this. We are producing software that will have in its virtual hands the lives of the occupants of the car, and the lives of those in other nearby cars, and the lives of nearby pedestrians, etc. Chess is not usually a life-or-death matter.

Driving is all around us. Cars are everywhere. Most of today's AI applications involve only a small number of people. Or, they are behind the scenes and we as humans have other recourse if the AI messes up. AI that is driving a car at 80 miles per hour on a highway had better not mess up. The consequences are grave. Multiply this by the number of cars, if we could put magically self-driving into every car in the USA, we'd have AI running in the 263 million cars. That's a lot of AI spread around. This is AI on a massive scale that we are not doing today and that offers both promise and potential peril.

There are some that want AI for self-driving cars because they envision a world without any car accidents. They envision a world in which there is no car congestion and all cars cooperate with each other. These are wonderful utopian visions.

They are also very misleading. The adoption of self-driving cars is going to be incremental and not overnight. We cannot economically just junk all existing cars. Nor are we going to be able to affordably retrofit existing cars. It is more likely that self-driving cars will be built into new cars and that over many years of gradual replacement of existing cars that we'll see the mix of self-driving cars become substantial in the real-world.

In these essays, I have tried to offer technological insights without being overly technical in my description, and also blended the business, societal, and economic aspects too. Technologists need to consider the non-technological impacts of what they do. Non-technologists should be aware of what is being developed.

We all need to work together to collectively be prepared for the enormous disruption and transformative aspects of true self-driving cars. We all need to be involved in this mother of all AI projects.

WHAT THIS BOOK PROVIDES

What does this book provide to you? It introduces many of the key elements about self-driving cars and does so with an AI based perspective. I weave together technical and non-technical aspects, readily going from being concerned about the cognitive capabilities of the driving task and how the technology is embodying this into self-driving cars, and in the next breath I discuss the societal and economic aspects.

They are all intertwined because that's the way reality is. You cannot separate out the technology per se, and instead must consider it within the milieu of what is being invented and innovated, and do so with a mindset towards the contemporary mores and culture that shape what we are doing and what we hope to do.

WHY THIS BOOK

I wrote this book to try and bring to the public view many aspects about self-driving cars that nobody seems to be discussing.

For business leaders that are either involved in making self-driving cars or that are going to leverage self-driving cars, I hope that this book will enlighten you as to the risks involved and ways in which you should be strategizing about how to deal with those risks.

For entrepreneurs, startups and other businesses that want to enter into the self-driving car market that is emerging, I hope this book sparks your interest in doing so, and provides some sense of what might be prudent to pursue.

For researchers that study self-driving cars, I hope this book spurs your interest in the risks and safety issues of self-driving cars, and also nudges you toward conducting research on those aspects.

For students in computer science or related disciplines, I hope this book will provide you with interesting and new ideas and material, for which you might conduct research or provide some career direction insights for you.

For AI companies and high-tech companies pursuing self-driving cars, this book will hopefully broaden your view beyond just the mere coding and development needed to make self-driving cars.

For all readers, I hope that you will find the material in this book to be stimulating. Some of it will be repetitive of things you already know. But I am pretty sure that you'll also find various eureka moments whereby you'll discover a new technique or approach that you had not earlier thought of. I am also betting that there will be material that forces you to rethink some of your current practices.

I am not saying you will suddenly have an epiphany and change what you are doing. I do think though that you will reconsider or perhaps revisit what you are doing.

For anyone choosing to use this book for teaching purposes, please take a look at my suggestions for doing so, as described in the Appendix. I have found the material handy in courses that I have taught, and likewise other faculty have told me that they have found the material handy, in some cases as extended readings and in other instances as a core part of their course (depending on the nature of the class).

In my writing for this book, I have tried carefully to blend both the practitioner and the academic styles of writing. It is not as dense as is typical academic journal writing, but at the same time offers depth by going into the nuances and trade-offs of various practices.

The word "deep" is in vogue today, meaning getting deeply into a subject or topic, and so is the word "unpack" which means to tease out the underlying aspects of a subject or topic. I have sought to offer material that addresses an issue or topic by going relatively deeply into it and make sure that it is well unpacked.

Finally, in any book about AI, it is difficult to use our everyday words without having some of them be misinterpreted. Specifically, it is easy to anthropomorphize AI. When I say that an AI system "knows" something, I do not want you to construe that the AI system has sentience and "knows" in the same way that humans do. They aren't that way, as yet. I have tried to use quotes around such words from time-to-time to emphasize that the words I am using should not be misinterpreted to ascribe true human intelligence to the AI systems that we know of today. If I used quotes around all such words, the book would be very difficult to read, and so I am doing so judiciously. Please keep that in mind as you read the material, thanks.

COMPANION BOOKS

If you find this material of interest, you might want to also see my other three books on self-driving cars, entitled:

- **"Innovation and Thought Leadership on Self-Driving Driverless Cars"** by Dr. Lance Eliot

- **"Advances in AI and Autonomous Vehicles: Cybernetic Self-Driving Cars"** by Dr. Lance Eliot

- ***"Self-Driving Cars: The Mother of All AI Projects"*** by Dr. Lance Eliot

- **"New Advances in AI Autonomous Driverless Self-Driving Cars"** by Dr. Lance Eliot

All of the above books are available on Amazon and at other major global booksellers.

Dr. Lance Eliot and Michael B. Eliot

14

CHAPTER 1

ELIOT FRAMEWORK FOR AI SELF-DRIVING CARS

Dr. Lance Eliot and Michael B. Eliot

16

CHAPTER 1

ELIOT FRAMEWORK FOR AI SELF-DRIVING CARS

When I give presentations about self-driving cars and teach classes on the topic, I have found it helpful to provide a framework around which the various key elements of self-driving cars can be understood and organized (see diagram at the end of this chapter). The framework needs to be simple enough to convey the overarching elements, but at the same time not so simple that it belies the true complexity of self-driving cars. As such, I am going to describe the framework here and try to offer in a thousand words (or more!) what the framework diagram itself intends to portray.

The core elements on the diagram are numbered for ease of reference. The numbering does not suggest any kind of prioritization of the elements. Each element is crucial. Each element has a purpose, and otherwise would not be included in the framework. For some self-driving cars, a particular element might be more important or somehow distinguished in comparison to other self-driving cars. You could even use the framework to rate a particular self-driving car, doing so by gauging how well it performs in each of the elements of the framework.

I will describe each of the elements, one at a time. After doing so, I'll discuss aspects that illustrate how the elements interact and perform during the overall effort of a self-driving car.

––––––––––

At the Cybernetic Self-Driving Car Institute, we use the framework to keep track of what we are working on, and how we are developing software that fills in what is needed to achieve Level 5 self-driving cars.

D-01: Sensor Capture

Let's start with the one element that often gets the most attention in the press about self-driving cars, namely, the sensory devices for a self-driving car.

On the framework, the box labeled as D-01 indicates "Sensor Capture" and refers to the processes of the self-driving car that involve collecting data from the myriad of sensors that are used for a self-driving car. The types of devices typically involved are listed, such as the use of mono cameras, stereo cameras, LIDAR devices, radar systems, ultrasonic devices, GPS, IMU, and so on.

These devices are tasked with obtaining data about the status of the self-driving car and the world around it. Some of the devices are continually providing updates, while others of the devices await an indication by the self-driving car that the device is supposed to collect data. The data might be first transformed in some fashion by the device itself, or it might instead be fed directly into the sensor capture as raw data. At that point, it might be up to the sensor capture processes to do transformations on the data. This all varies depending upon the nature of the devices being used and how the devices were designed and developed.

D-02: Sensor Fusion

Imagine that your eyeballs receive visual images, your nose receives odors, your ears receive sounds, and in essence each of your distinct sensory devices is getting some form of input. The input befits the nature of the device. Likewise, for a self-driving car, the cameras provide visual images, the radar returns radar reflections, and so on. Each device provides the data as befits what the device does.

At some point, using the analogy to humans, you need to merge together what your eyes see, what your nose smells, what your ears hear, and piece it all together into a larger sense of what the world is all about and what is happening around you. Sensor fusion is the action of taking the singular aspects from each of the devices and putting them together into a larger puzzle.

Sensor fusion is a tough task. There are some devices that might not be working at the time of the sensor capture. Or, there might some devices that are unable to report well what they have detected. Again, using a human analogy, suppose you are in a dark room and so your eyes cannot see much. At that point, you might need to rely more so on your ears and what you hear. The same is true for a self-driving car. If the cameras are obscured due to snow and sleet, it might be that the radar can provide a greater indication of what the external conditions consist of.

In the case of a self-driving car, there can be a plethora of such sensory devices. Each is reporting what it can. Each might have its difficulties. Each might have its limitations, such as how far ahead it can detect an object. All of these limitations need to be considered during the sensor fusion task.

D-03: Virtual World Model

For humans, we presumably keep in our minds a model of the world around us when we are driving a car. In your mind, you know that the car is going at say 60 miles per hour and that you are on a freeway. You have a model in your mind that your car is surrounded by other cars, and that there are lanes to the freeway. Your model is not only based on what you can see, hear, etc., but also what you know about the nature of the world. You know that at any moment that car ahead of you can smash on its brakes, or the car behind you can ram into your car, or that the truck in the next lane might swerve into your lane.

The AI of the self-driving car needs to have a virtual world model, which it then keeps updated with whatever it is receiving from the sensor fusion, which received its input from the sensor capture and the sensory devices.

D-04: System Action Plan

By having a virtual world model, the AI of the self-driving car is able to keep track of where the car is and what is happening around the car. In addition, the AI needs to determine what to do next. Should the self-driving car hit its brakes? Should the self-driving car stay in its lane or swerve into the lane to the left? Should the self-driving car accelerate or slow down?

A system action plan needs to be prepared by the AI of the self-driving car. The action plan specifies what actions should be taken. The actions need to pertain to the status of the virtual world model. Plus, the actions need to be realizable.

This realizability means that the AI cannot just assert that the self-driving car should suddenly sprout wings and fly. Instead, the AI must be bound by whatever the self-driving car can actually do, such as coming to a halt in a distance of X feet at a speed of Y miles per hour, rather than perhaps asserting that the self-driving car come to a halt in 0 feet as though it could instantaneously come to a stop while it is in motion.

D-05: Controls Activation

The system action plan is implemented by activating the controls of the car to act according to what the plan stipulates. This might mean that the accelerator control is commanded to increase the speed of the car. Or, the steering control is commanded to turn the steering wheel 30 degrees to the left or right.

One question arises as to whether or not the controls respond as they are commanded to do. In other words, suppose the AI has commanded the accelerator to increase, but for some reason it does not do so. Or, maybe it tries to do so, but the speed of the car does not increase. The controls activation feeds back into the virtual world model, and simultaneously the virtual world model is getting updated from the sensors, the sensor capture, and the sensor fusion. This allows the AI to ascertain what has taken place as a result of the controls being commanded to take some kind of action.

By the way, please keep in mind that though the diagram seems to have a linear progression to it, the reality is that these are all aspects of the self-driving car that are happening in parallel and simultaneously. The sensors are capturing data, meanwhile the sensor fusion is taking place, meanwhile the virtual model is being updated, meanwhile the system action plan is being formulated and reformulated, meanwhile the controls are being activated.

This is the same as a human being that is driving a car. They are eyeballing the road, meanwhile they are fusing in their mind the sights, sounds, etc., meanwhile their mind is updating their model of the world around them, meanwhile they are formulating an action plan of what to do, and meanwhile they are pushing their foot onto the pedals and steering the car. In the normal course of driving a car, you are doing all of these at once. I mention this so that when you look at the diagram, you will think of the boxes as processes that are all happening at the same time, and not as though only one happens and then the next.

They are shown diagrammatically in a simplistic manner to help comprehend what is taking place. You though should also realize that they are working in parallel and simultaneous with each other. This is a tough aspect in that the inter-element communications involve latency and other aspects that must be taken into account. There can be delays in one element updating and then sharing its latest status with other elements.

D-06: Automobile & CAN

Contemporary cars use various automotive electronics and a Controller Area Network (CAN) to serve as the components that underlie the driving aspects of a car. There are Electronic Control Units (ECU's) which control subsystems of the car, such as the engine, the brakes, the doors, the windows, and so on.

The elements D-01, D-02, D-03, D-04, D-05 are layered on top of the D-06, and must be aware of the nature of what the D-06 is able to do and not do.

D-07: In-Car Commands

Humans are going to be occupants in self-driving cars. In a Level 5 self-driving car, there must be some form of communication that takes place between the humans and the self-driving car. For example, I go into a self-driving car and tell it that I want to be driven over to Disneyland, and along the way I want to stop at In-and-Out Burger. The self-driving car now parses what I've said and tries to then establish a means to carry out my wishes.

In-car commands can happen at any time during a driving journey. Though my example was about an in-car command when I first got into my self-driving car, it could be that while the self-driving car is carrying out the journey that I change my mind. Perhaps after getting stuck in traffic, I tell the self-driving car to forget about getting the burgers and just head straight over to the theme park. The self-driving car needs to be alert to in-car commands throughout the journey.

D-08: VX2 Communications

We will ultimately have self-driving cars communicating with each other, doing so via V2V (Vehicle-to-Vehicle) communications. We will also have self-driving cars that communicate with the roadways and other aspects of the transportation infrastructure, doing so via V2I (Vehicle-to-Infrastructure).

The variety of ways in which a self-driving car will be communicating with other cars and infrastructure is being called V2X, whereby the letter X means whatever else we identify as something that a car should or would want to communicate with. The V2X communications will be taking place simultaneous with everything else on the diagram, and those other elements will need to incorporate whatever it gleans from those V2X communications.

D-09: Deep Learning

The use of Deep Learning permeates all other aspects of the self-driving car. The AI of the self-driving car will be using deep learning to do a better job at the systems action plan, and at the controls activation, and at the sensor fusion, and so on.

Currently, the use of artificial neural networks is the most prevalent form of deep learning. Based on large swaths of data, the neural networks attempt to "learn" from the data and therefore direct the efforts of the self-driving car accordingly.

D-10: Tactical AI

Tactical AI is the element of dealing with the moment-to-moment driving of the self-driving car. Is the self-driving car staying in its lane of the freeway? Is the car responding appropriately to the controls commands? Are the sensory devices working?

For human drivers, the tactical equivalent can be seen when you watch a novice driver such as a teenager that is first driving. They are focused on the mechanics of the driving task, keeping their eye on the road while also trying to properly control the car.

D-11: Strategic AI

The Strategic AI aspects of a self-driving car are dealing with the larger picture of what the self-driving car is trying to do. If I had asked that the self-driving car take me to Disneyland, there is an overall journey map that needs to be kept and maintained.

There is an interaction between the Strategic AI and the Tactical AI. The Strategic AI is wanting to keep on the mission of the driving, while the Tactical AI is focused on the particulars underway in the driving effort. If the Tactical AI seems to wander away from the overarching mission, the Strategic AI wants to see why and get things back on track. If the Tactical AI realizes that there is something amiss on the self-driving car, it needs to alert the Strategic AI accordingly and have an adjustment to the overarching mission that is underway.

D-12: Self-Aware AI

Very few of the self-driving cars being developed are including a Self-Aware AI element, which we at the Cybernetic Self-Driving Car Institute believe is crucial to Level 5 self-driving cars.

The Self-Aware AI element is intended to watch over itself, in the sense that the AI is making sure that the AI is working as intended. Suppose you had a human driving a car, and they were starting to drive erratically. Hopefully, their own self-awareness would make them realize they themselves are driving poorly, such as perhaps starting to fall asleep after having been driving for hours on end. If you had a passenger in the car, they might be able to alert the driver if the driver is starting to do something amiss. This is exactly what the Self-Aware AI element tries to do, it becomes the overseer of the AI, and tries to detect when the AI has become faulty or confused, and then find ways to overcome the issue.

D-13: Economic

The economic aspects of a self-driving car are not per se a technology aspect of a self-driving car, but the economics do indeed impact the nature of a self-driving car. For example, the cost of outfitting a self-driving car with every kind of possible sensory device is prohibitive, and so choices need to be made about which devices are used. And, for those sensory devices chosen, whether they would have a full set of features or a more limited set of features.

We are going to have self-driving cars that are at the low-end of a consumer cost point, and others at the high-end of a consumer cost point. You cannot expect that the self-driving car at the low-end is going to be as robust as the one at the high-end. I realize that many of the self-driving car pundits are acting as though all self-driving cars will be the same, but they won't be. Just like anything else, we are going to have self-driving cars that have a range of capabilities. Some will be better than others. Some will be safer than others. This is the way of the real-world, and so we need to be thinking about the economics aspects when considering the nature of self-driving cars.

D-14: Societal

The societal aspects also impact the technology of self-driving car. For example, the famous Trolley Problem involves what choices should a self-driving car make when faced with life-and-death matters. If the self-driving car is about to either hit a child standing in the roadway, or instead ram into a tree at the side of the road and possibly kill the humans in the self-driving car, which choice should be made?

We need to keep in mind the societal aspects will underlie the AI of the self-driving car. Whether we are aware of it explicitly or not, the AI will have embedded into it various societal assumptions.

D-15: Innovation

I included the notion of innovation into the framework because we can anticipate that whatever a self-driving car consists of, it will continue to be innovated over time. The self-driving cars coming out in the next several years will undoubtedly be different and less innovative than the versions that come out in ten years hence, and so on.

Framework Overall

For those of you that want to learn about self-driving cars, you can potentially pick a particular element and become specialized in that aspect. Some engineers are focusing on the sensory devices. Some engineers focus on the controls activation. And so on. There are specialties in each of the elements.

Researchers are likewise specializing in various aspects. For example, there are researchers that are using Deep Learning to see how best it can be used for sensor fusion. There are other researchers that are using Deep Learning to derive good System Action Plans. Some are studying how to develop AI for the Strategic aspects of the driving task, while others are focused on the Tactical aspects.

A well-prepared all-around software developer that is involved in self-driving cars should be familiar with all of the elements, at least to the degree that they know what each element does. This is important since whatever piece of the pie that the software developer works on, they need to be knowledgeable about what the other elements are doing.

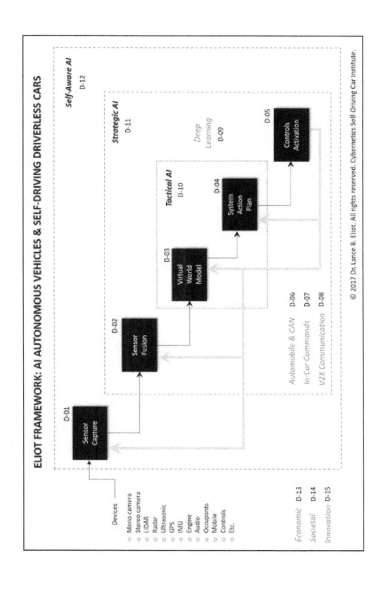

Dr. Lance Eliot and Michael B. Eliot

CHAPTER 2

ROCKET MAN DRIVERS AND AI SELF-DRIVING CARS

CHAPTER 2

ROCKET MAN DRIVERS AND AI SELF-DRIVING CARS

I was on the freeway the other day and traffic was moving along rather smoothly. Even though there were quite a number of cars on the road, we were all doing a steady 55 miles per hour. That's an accomplishment in the crowded freeways of Southern California. Some days I get maybe an average speed of 10 miles per hour during commute times, and often it drops to around 5 miles per hour on the average. Whenever the freeway moves along at a fast clip, I look around wondering if maybe the end of the earth is nearly upon us, or some other miracle has occurred that no one bothered to tell me about.

Well, there I am, enjoying my speedy 55 miles per hour, when in my rear view mirror I spot a Rocket Man. When I say Rocket Man, I am generically referring to any human driver that decides they are going to rocket through traffic. It could be a man or a woman, and I just use "Rocket Man" because it is a handy and catchy term for the behavior. Please think of it as Rocket Person.

I could see the car about a quarter mile behind me. It was moving forward at a fast pace, probably doing at least 20 to 30 miles an hour faster speed than the prevailing traffic. I would guess that the car was going around 85 to 90 miles per hour. This might be Okay if the driver was on a straightaway that had no traffic, but instead this driver was doing that kind of speed while weaving into and around other cars. The offending car would zip ahead in the fast lane, come upon a

31

"slow" car that was doing the 55 miles per hour of the rest of us, and then dive into the lane to the right when there was an opening.

The driver would then zip forward in that lane, and was looking to make the next jump to another lane, since the driver had reached the bumper of a car in the existing lane and was now blocked from going at the 90 miles per hour clip. Into and out of the other lanes of traffic and narrowly missing hitting other cars was the pattern of driving behavior. The wild driver would almost always come right up to the bumper of a car in whatever lane the wild driver was in and then in a semi-panic mode desperately try to switch lanes. It was a very dangerous effort. The speeding driver would muscle into another lane and cause the cars in that lane to slow down to let in the wild driver.

I am sure that in the mind of the wild driver that he or she perceived the rest of us as sheep. We were just abiding by traffic flow, and this other driver figured why be so sheepish. Instead, this aggressive driver figured that they would try to tie together any possible openings and jump from one to the other. I am further guessing that the wild driver didn't think this was particularly dangerous. They probably thought it was perfectly fine as a driving strategy. I've spoken to such drivers and they claim too that they are actually helping traffic. They think that they are optimizing the available driving space by using it in this fashion. No sense in leaving any gaps or openings, they figure, and instead maximize traffic flow by having cars in all available roadway space.

Of course, that's a crock.

This Rocket Man driver is putting all other drivers at a heightened risk of injury or death. Their wild antics can easily cause an accident to occur. This can happen by their direct actions such as they ram into a car and cause the accident to happen. It can also occur by their indirect actions, such that if the rest of traffic is trying to adjust to this nutty behavior, you can have innocent cars that get caught into a domino effect that leads to car crashes. In other words, if car W, the wild driver, cuts off a driver X, and then driver X hits their brakes, but driver Y behind driver X wasn't expecting it, and then driver X and Y hit each other, the driver W can pretend they had nothing to do with it.

Some of these knuckle head drivers will even insist that if other cars get into an accident because of their rude behavior, it merely shows that those other drivers are bad drivers and should not be on the freeways. The wild driver believes that other drivers should be watching out for them, and it is not the wild driver that needs to be on alert. All I'm doing is weaving into and out of traffic, the Rocket Man says, and if other drivers are so stupid that they can't handle it, they deserve to get into a wreck.

I often wish that I had some instant means to inform the police about such drivers. You look around and hopelessly wish that a highway patrol car will be on the freeway and spot such a driver. I almost never see these drivers getting caught. I'd like to pretend that they do. I'd like to pretend that their behavior is so frequent that they ultimately are getting caught. But, unfortunately, I would realistically guess that it is somewhat rare that they get caught. Getting caught is not especially likely since these wild drivers are usually watching for the cops, and they try to turn innocent when they see the police. Once the police are no longer around, they continue their wild driving.

Furthermore, it would be difficult for a highway patrol car to realize what is going on. If the wild driver was on a straightaway and doing 90 miles per hour, a highway patrol car could easily see that the driver was speeding and observe as such over a clear-cut distance. Instead, by weaving in and out of traffic, the wild driver is actually somewhat obscured and hidden from view. Only if you were observing from above, such as being in a police helicopter or plane, could you readily see the pattern of the driver and realize they are driving recklessly and at high speeds.

Some of these wild drivers do other illegal acts too. They will often dart into and out of the car pool lanes, even though they are not legally allowed to do so. They will often make use of the emergency lane as though it is a conventional lane, committing another illegal act. They will often intimidate other cars and pretty much chase them, and take other actions that are totally abusive of the privileges of being able to drive a car. You might say that their weaving into and out of traffic is really just a microcosm on their overall bad behavior as a driver. They are likely drivers that have disdain for the civilized rules of driving, and we merely happen to witness more clearly their disdain when they act in these aggressive manners.

That being said, there are certainly some instances of the normal everyday driver that opts to drive in a Rocket Man like way. If you are late for work and worried about losing your job, you're likely to adopt that same bad practice that day or that moment. Or, if you are maybe in a joyful playful mood, you might think it is fun to momentarily try to weave in and out of traffic. It becomes almost like a personal game of Frogger. Though, you are at risk of bodily harm due to driving a motor vehicle at high speeds, and others around you are also at heightened risk, you nonetheless treat driving like a game at times. When behind the wheel of a car, we all sometimes forget that we are in a killing machine and can become distanced from reality by acting as though we are in some gigantic video game.

What does this have to do with AI self-driving cars?

At the Cybernetic Self-Driving Car Institute, we are developing AI that takes into account the Rocket Man drivers and can undertake various evasive actions accordingly. Furthermore, the self-driving car can become a Rocket Man, if needed, by using the same techniques that we generally don't want cars to do (more on this in a moment).

First, let's discuss how to detect that a car is driving in a Rocket Man way.

The sensory devices of the self-driving car should be looking behind the self-driving car and up ahead in front of the driving car. These might be a combination of LIDAR, cameras, ultra-sonic, etc. By analyzing the sensory data, what we are looking for is car behavior outside the norm. If the norm of the traffic at the time of analysis is that most of the cars are doing speed A, and if a car is doing a much faster speed B, we want to flag internally that as a car to be further closely observed. It stands out among the rest of the traffic.

This car B could be making a one-time sudden lane change and thus it is not truly a Rocket Man. Thus, we need to watch over time to see whether a car is consistently acting as a Rocket Man. It usually doesn't take much time to ascertain the behavior. The biggest problem is usually being able to track the Rocket Man candidate. There are likely other cars and trucks on the freeway that obscure the wild driver. This is especially the case due to the wild driver weaving into and out of lanes. Imagine it is like playing a game of hide-and-seek. One moment, you can see the wild car, the next moment is seems to disappear.

Our main criteria is the speed differential in comparison to the other traffic, combined with the rapid lane changes, combined with the narrow gaps between cars. The Rocket Man has a tendency to run right up to the bumper of other cars. In their little minds, they think that this is the optimum way to make forward progress. If they were to study simulations, which we've done extensively, they would find out that their bumper nearing antics is actually not the fastest way to skirt through traffic. Had they a more open mind, they might realize that a more optimal path is possible, but most of the time they are just doing a monkey-see monkey-do kind of driving practice.

In fact, in some of our testing on the roads, we've been able to move ahead at a faster pace than the average Rocket Man, by adopting the same principles but performing the actions in a more studied manner. The act of changing lanes and weaving can be done with grace and aplomb, while the crasser approach is not only more dangerous but not even necessarily as successful. In essence, sometimes weaving across all four lanes of traffic, though it might seem like a faster way to proceed, can be beat by for example weaving only within two lanes of traffic. It involves lining up the weaving opportunities and timing them just right.

You might be wondering why I am describing this driving behavior as wild and yet at the same time touting there are better ways to do it. Am I being inconsistent? Nope. The reason why it is useful to do this kind of driving in a better way is related to the future of driving. Eventually, some believe that the roadways will have only self-driving cars (there won't be any human driven cars). Though it is questionable that this will happen, let's go with the assumption for the moment.

If all cars on the freeway are self-driving cars, they can potentially coordinate their movements. It will be like a herd or a swam of animals that work in unison with each other. As such, the overall pace for all of the self-driving cars can be heightened by working together. This might also involve allowing some cars to do the Rocket Man like behavior. Suppose that the freeway is filled with self-driving cars, all moving along at some normal speed, and then one of the self-driving cars has an emergency, such as a human occupant that has had a heart attack. We might want that self-driving car to then perform Rocket Man maneuvers to allow it to proceed ahead at a faster pace than the rest of the traffic.

I realize that some of you that are cynics will say that you'd want your self-driving car to always be the Rocket Man, and thus move faster than the rest of the traffic. But, of course, if all the self-driving cars did this, we'd not really end-up moving any faster. All in all, we will likely ultimately have new driving regulations that will indicate when self-driving cars are to behave like the rest of traffic, and when they can do individualized acts such as a Rocket Man (such as the heart attack example of an occupant).

It is for these above reasons that we not only are developing AI to cope with the human driven Rocket Man behavior, but also want the AI of the self-driving car to be able to drive like a Rocket Man. The Rocket Man skill is worthwhile for the AI to have available. This does not mean that it is skill that should be used, and presumably would only be used when appropriate.

Let's get back to the detection of human driven Rocket Man behavior.

Once the sensory data has been examined and we've detected a potential Rocket Man, the virtual model of the driving world is then updated to flag that car. We can then begin to predict what that car will do next. Based on the prediction, the self-driving car AI can take a defensive posture.

For example, if the Rocket Man is coming up from behind the self-driving car, the AI can opt to switch lanes if that will help avoid having the Rocket Man get onto the bumper of the self-driving car. The AI might opt to slow down, or speed-up, depending upon which approach is best for the circumstance. Generally, the AI is trying to avoid the Rocket Man from ramming into the self-driving car.

I've seen some human drivers that have either unintentionally or intentionally cut-off a Rocket Man driver. This can anger the Rocket Man driver and make them do even worse things. The Rocket Man will sometimes purposely get in front of a car that cut them off, and then play a dangerous game of braking to make the other car get scared. This of course actually slows down the progress of the Rocket Man, but they often seem to be of such a mired mind that seeking revenge is apparently more important than speeding ahead.

If necessary, the AI of the self-driving car might even opt to take the self-driving car off the freeway entirely, for the moment, and allow the Rocket Man to proceed on their way. It all depends on how desperately the Rocket Man seems to be driving and the predicted danger to the self-driving car and its occupants.

Speaking of the occupants of the self-driving car, we also have the AI inform the occupants about the Rocket Man, if appropriate to do so. This is based on whether the occupants have indicated to the AI that they want to be kept informed about the traffic conditions. On the one hand, the AI does not want to needlessly panic the occupants, while at the same time if the AI is going to be taking evasive maneuvers then the occupants might be wondering and concerned as to why the self-driving car is taking such actions.

Once we have self-driving cars that are communicating with each other via V2V (vehicle to vehicle) communications, the AI could inform other cars to be watchful of the Rocket Man. This would aid other self-driving cars that have not yet detected the Rocket Man, or that have software that is not as advanced that is able to detect Rocket Man behavior. Likewise, if self-driving cars are able to communicate externally, they could potentially alert the police – which then takes us to my earlier point about wanting to let the cops know when a driver of this ilk is on the roadway.

I have been describing the Rocket Man as a lone wolf driver. There is nothing that precludes there being multiple Rocket Man drivers at the same time. Indeed, I see this during my daily commute. There are often several Rocket Man drivers all vying to get ahead in the traffic. The AI therefore needs to be able to handle the one-at-time circumstance and the gaggle of Rocket Man drivers too.

CHAPTER 3

OCCAM'S RAZOR CRUCIAL FOR AI SELF-DRIVING CARS

CHAPTER 3

OCCAM'S RAZOR CRUCIAL FOR AI SELF-DRIVING CARS

Let me begin by saying that I believe in Occam's razor. A variant is also known as Zebra. I'll explain all of this in a moment, but first, a bit of a preamble to warm you up for the rest of the story.

Self-driving cars are complex.

Besides all of the various automotive parts and vehicular components that would be needed for any conventional car, a self-driving car is also loaded down with dozens of specialized sensory devices, potentially hundreds of microprocessors, ECU's, online storage devices, a myriad of communications devices within the vehicle and for internal and external communications, and so on. It's a veritable bazaar of electronic and computational elements. Imagine the latest NASA rocket ship or an advanced jet fighter plane, and you are starting to see the magnitude of what is within the scope of a true self-driving car.

The big question is whether or not the complexity will undermine achieving a true self-driving car.

That's right, I dared to say that we might be heading toward a system that becomes so complex that it either won't work, or it will work but will have serious and potentially lethal problems, or that it might work but do so in a manner that no one can really know whether it has hidden within it some fatal flaw that will reveal itself at the worst

41

of times.

I am not seeking to be alarmist. I am just pointing out that we are moving forward with conventional cars and adding more and more complexity onto them. There are some auto designers that think we are building a skyscraper onto the top of a tall building and so we are asking for trouble. They believe that self-driving cars should go back to the beginning and from the ground-up redesign what a car consists of. In that sense, they believe that we need to reinvent the car, doing so with the guise of what we desire a self-driving car to be able to do.

This is a very important and serious point. Right now, there are some auto makers and tech companies that are making add-ons for conventional cars that will presumably turn them into self-driving cars. Most of the auto makers and tech companies are integrating specialized systems into conventional cars to produce self-driving cars. Almost no one is taking the route of restarting altogether what a car should be and from scratch making it into a self-driving car (this is mainly an experimental or research approach).

It makes sense that we would want to just add a self-driving car capability onto what we already can do with conventional cars. Rather than starting with nothing, why not use what we already have. We know that conventional cars work. If you try to start over, you face two daunting challenges, namely making a car that works and then also making it be self-driving. From a cost perspective, it is less expensive to toss onto a conventional car the self-driving car capabilities. From a time factor, it is faster to take that same approach. A blank slate approach for developing a self-driving car is going to take a lot longer to get to market. Besides, who would be able to support such a car, including getting parts for it, etc.

That being said, a few contrarians say that we will never be able to graft onto a conventional car the needed capabilities to make a true Level 5 self-driving car. They argue that the auto makers and tech companies will perhaps achieve a Level 4 self-driving car, but then get stymied and unable to make it to a Level 5. Meanwhile, those working in their garages and research labs that took the route of starting from scratch will suddenly become the limelight of Level 5 achievement.

They will have labored all those years in the darkness without any accolades, and maybe even have faced ridicule for their quiet efforts, and suddenly find themselves the heroes of getting us to Level 5.

Let's though get back to the focus here, which is that self-driving cars are getting increasingly complex. We are barely into Level 2 and Level 3, and already self-driving cars have gone up nearly exponentially in complexity. Level 4 is presumably another lurch upward. Level 5, well, we're not sure how high up that might be in terms of complexity.

Why does complexity matter? As mentioned earlier, with immense complexity it becomes harder and harder to ascertain whether a self-driving car will work as intended. The testing that is done prior to putting the self-driving car on the road can only get you so far. The number of paths and variations of what a self-driving car and the AI will do is huge, and lab based testing is only going to uncover a fraction of whatever weaknesses or bugs might lurk within the system.

The complexity gets even more obscured due to the machine learning aspects of the AI and the self-driving car. Test the self-driving car and AI as much as you like, but the moment it is driving on the roads, it is already changing. The learning aspects will lead to the system doing something differently than what you had earlier tested. A self-driving car with one hundred hours of roadway time is going to be quite different from the same self-driving car that has only one hour of roadway time. For those AI systems using neural networks, the neural network connections, weights, and the like, will be changing as the self-driving car collects more data and gleans more experiences under actual driving conditions and situations.

When a self-driving car and its AI goes awry, how will the developers identify the source of the problem? The complexity of interaction between the sensory devices, the sensor fusion, the strategic AI driving elements, the tactical AI driving elements, the ECU's, and the other aspect will confound and hide where the problem resides.

Let's say Zebra.

Allow me to explain.

In the medical domain, they have a saying known as "Zebra" that traces back to the 1940's when Dr. Theodore Woodward at the University of Maryland told interns: "When you hear hoofbeats, think of horses, not zebras." What he was trying to convey was that when trying to do a medical diagnosis, the interns often were looking for the most obscure of medical illnesses to accommodate the diagnosis.

Patient has a runny nose, fever, and rashes on their neck, this might be the rare Zamboni disease that only one-hundredth of one percent of people get. Hogwash, one might say. It is just someone with the common cold. Dr. Woodward emphasized that in Maryland, if you hear the sounds of hoofs, the odds are much higher that it is a horse, than if it were a zebra (about the only chance of it being a zebra is if you were at the Maryland zoo).

For a self-driving car, and when it has a problem, which for sure they will have problems, the question will be whether it is something obvious that has gone astray, or whether it is something buried deep within a tiny component hidden within a stack of fifty other components. The inherent complexity of self-driving cars is going to make it hard to know. Will the sound of a hoofbeat mean it is a horse or is it a zebra? We won't have the same kind of statistical bases to go on, unlike the medical domain and knowing what the likelihood of various illnesses are.

At the Cybernetic Self-Driving Car Institute, we are developing AI self-driving software and trying to abide by Occam's razor as we do so.

Occam's razor is a well-known principle that derives from the notion that simplicity matters. In the sciences, many times there have been occasions of theories that were developed to explain some phenomena of nature, and those theories were quite complex. If someone could derive a similar theory that was simpler, and yet still provided the same explanation, it was considered that the simpler version was the better version. As Einstein emphasized: "Everything should be kept as simple as possible, but no simpler."

William of Ockham in the early 1300's had put forth long before Einstein that among competing hypotheses, whichever hypothesis has the least number of assumptions ought to be the winning hypothesis. In his own words, he had said: "Entities are not to be multiplied without necessity" (translated from the Latin of non sunt multiplicanda entia sine necessitate). The razor part of Occam's razor is that he advocated essentially reducing or shaving away at assumptions until you got to the barest set needed. By the way, it is permitted to say that it is Ockham's razor, if you want to abide closely to the spelling of his proper name, but by widespread acceptance it is usually indicated as Occam's razor.

You can go even further back in time and attribute this same important concept to Aristotle. Based on translation, he had said that: "Nature operates in the shortest way possible." If that's not enough for you, he also was known for this: "We may assume the superiority ceteris paribus (other things being equal) of the demonstration which derives from fewer postulates or hypotheses." Overall, there have been quite a number of well-known scientists, philosophers, architects, designers, and others that have warned about the dangers of over-complicating things.

For those of you that are AI developers, you likely already know that Bayesian inference, an important aspect of dealing with probabilities in AI systems, also makes use of the same Occam's razor principle. Indeed, we already recognize that with each introduction of another variable or assumption, it increases the potential for added errors. You can also look to the Turing machine as a kind of Occam's razor. The Turing machine makes use of a minimal set of instructions. Presumably enough to be able to have a useful construct, but no more so than needed to achieve it.

In the realm of machine learning and neural networks, it is important to be mindful of Occam's razor. I say this because with large data sets and at times mindless attempts to use massive neural networks to identify and catch onto patterns, there is the danger of doing overfitting. The complex neural network can possibly be impacted by statistical noise in the data. A less complex neural network might actually do a better job of fit, and be more generalizable to other circumstances.

For a self-driving car, we need to be cognizant of Occam's razor.

The designers of the AI systems and the self-driving car should be continually assessing whether the complexity that they are shaping is absolutely necessary. Might there be a more parsimonious way to structure the system? Can you do the same actions with less code, or less modules, or otherwise reduce the size of the system?

Many of the self-driving car AI code has arisen from AI researchers and research labs. In those circumstances, the complexity hasn't particularly been a topic of concern. When you are first trying to see if you can construct something, it is likely to have all sorts of variants as you were experimenting with one aspect after another. Rather than carrying those variants into a self-driving car that is going to actually be on-the-road and in mass production, it is helpful and indeed crucial to take a step back and relook at it.

I've personally inspected a lot of open source code for self-driving cars that is the proverbial spaghetti code. This is programming code that has been written, rewritten, rewritten again, and after a multitude of tries finally gotten to work. Within the morass, there is something that works. But, it is hidden and obscured by the other aspects that are no longer genuinely needed. Taking the time to prune it is worthy to do. Of course, there are some that would say if it works, leave it alone. Only touch those things that are broken.

If you are under pressure to get the AI software going for a self-driving car, admittedly you aren't going to be motivated to clean-up your code and make it simpler and more pristine. All you care about is getting it to work. There's an old saying in the programming profession, you don't need to have style in a street fight. Do whatever is needed to win the fight. As such, toiling night after night and day after day to get the AI for the self-driving car to work, it's hard to then also say let's make it simpler and wring out the complexity. No one is likely to care at the time. But, once it is in production, and once problems surface, there will be many that will care then, since the effort and time to debug and ferret out the problems, and find solutions, will be enormous.

There's another popular expression in the software field that applies to self-driving cars and the complexity of their AI systems. It's this, don't be paving the cow paths. This refers to the aspect that if you've ever been to Boston, you might have noticed that the streets there are crazily designed. There are one-way streets that zig and zag. Streets intersect with other streets in odds places and at strange angles. When you compare the streets in Boston to the design of the streets in New York, you begin to appreciate how New York City makes use of a grid shape and has avenues and streets that resemble an Excel spreadsheet type of shape.

How did Boston's streets get so oddly designed? The story is that during the early days of Boston, they would bring the cows into town. The cows would go whichever way that they wanted to go. They would weave here and there. The dirt roads were made by the cows wanting to go that way or this way. Then, later on, when cars started to come along, the easiest way to pave the streets was to use the dirt paths that had already been formulated essentially as streets. Thus, rather than redesigning, they just paved what had been there before.

Are we doing the same with the AI systems for self-driving cars? Rather than starting from scratch, though using what we now know about the needs and nature of such AI systems, are we better off to proceed as we are now, building upon building of what we have already forged? Doing so tends to push complexity up. We've seen that many believe that complexity should be reduced, if feasible, and that simpler is better.

You might be surprised to know that there is a counter movement to the Occam's razor, the anti-razors, which say that the razor proponents have put an undue focus on complexity, which they argue is pretty much a red herring. They cite many times in history where there was a movement toward a simpler explanation or simpler theory, and it backfired. Some point to theories of continental drift, and even theories about the atom, and emphasize that there were attempts to simplify that in the end were dead-ends and led us astray.

There are also those that question how you can even measure and determine complexity versus simplicity. If my AI software for a self-driving car has 50 modules, and yours has 100, does this ergo imply that mine is less complex than yours? Not really. It could be that I have 50 modules each of which is tremendously complex, while maybe you've flattened out the complexity and therefore have 100 modules. Or, of course, it could be the other way too, namely that I was able to reduce the 100 complex ones into 50 simpler ones.

We need to be careful about what we mean by the words complexity and simplicity. I know of many AI developers that say they know it when they see it. It's like art. Though this is catchy, it also should be pointed out that there are many well-developed software metrics that can help to identify complexity and we can use those as a straw man for trying to determine complexity versus simplicity in self-driving car systems.

For auto makers and tech companies that are designing, developing, and planning to field self-driving cars, I urge you to take a look at the nature of the complexity you are putting in place. It might not seem important now, but when those self-driving cars are on the roads, and when we begin to see problems emerge and cannot discern where in the system the problem sits, it could be the death knell of the self-driving car. I don't want to seem overly simplistic, but let's go with the notion that complexity equals bad, and simplicity equals good, assuming that all else is otherwise equal.

Now that I've said that, the anti-razors are going to be crying foul, and so let me augment my remarks. Sometimes complexity is bad, and simplicity is better, while sometimes complexity is good and simplicity is worse. Either way, you need to be cognizant of the roles of complexity and simplicity, and be aware of what you are doing. Don't fall blindly into complexity, and don't fall blindly into simplicity. Know what you are doing.

CHAPTER 4
SIMULTANEOUS LOCAL/MAP (SLAM) FOR SELF-DRIVING CARS

CHAPTER 4

SIMULATANEOUS LOCAL/MAP (SLAM)

FOR SELF-DRIVING CARS

Where am I?

I know that I am standing in a dark room. It is so dark that I cannot see anything at all. I was led into the room while wearing a blindfold. Once inside the room, I was walked around in a circuitous manner, making numerous loops, and also being turned around and around. This was intended to disorient me such that I would not have any sense of north or south, nor any sense of how large the room was, etc. The person that led me into the room was able to sneak out without revealing which direction they went. I had no idea where the door into the room was.

At this point, all I had was my sense of touch available. My eyes could not see anything because of the utter darkness. My ears would not do me much good, since there wasn't anything in here that was making any noise. I could speak or yell, not due to wanting help, but in hopes of using my own voice as a kind of echo locater. Perhaps my sounds would bounce off of objects in the room. Well, after trying this, I decided that apparently, I am not a bat. I don't seem to have much of an ability to echo locate objects.

I stretched out my arms. I gingerly began to move my feet. I decided that I should shuffle forward, very slowly, an inch at a time. There could be small objects laying on the floor. There could be large objects sitting in the room. If I had just started walking forward with abandon, I likely would collide with an object, possibly hurting me or damaging it. As I proceeded forward, I wondered how I would know if I had double backed on my own steps. In other words, I might think I am walking straight ahead, but maybe start to curve, and ultimately make a circle, which would bring me back to where I had started. It was so dark that I wouldn't know that I had done so.

I know that this all sounds kind of crazy. Though, if you are familiar with Escape Rooms, you might not think that this is very unusual. Escape Rooms have become popular recently. They are specially prepared rooms that you are placed into, for fun, and you need to solve various riddles and puzzles to find your way out. These Escape Rooms are usually done on a timed basis, and often done with a group of people. It can be a fun party-like experience. There is often a theme, such as you are in a bank vault and need to get out, or you are in a locked-room murder mystery and need to be like Sherlock Holmes to find clues, solve the murder, and escape from the room.

But that's not what I was doing.

Instead, I was pretending to be a robot.

Huh? You might wonder, what is Lance saying. He's become a robot? No, I said that I was pretending to be a robot.

There has been a great deal of study done of how robots can make sense of their environment. If a robot is placed into the middle of a room, and it has not been previously programmed with the particulars of the room and the objects in the room, it needs to have some means to figure out the layout of the room and the objects in the room. It is similar to a human being placed into a dark room that has no prior indication of what is in the room. Furthermore, the human doesn't even know the particulars of the room, such as how large it is, how many walls there are, and so on. That's the way a robot might be, since it might not have any previous indication of what the room is about.

I guess you could say it is a version of Escape Room for robots. Say, do you think the robot has fun while it tries to figure out the room?

Anyway, the robot would need to navigate in the room and gradually figure out as much as it can about the room and the objects in the room. This is a well-known and much studied problem in AI, robotics, and computer science, and it is more commonly referred to as SLAM, which is an acronym for Simultaneous Localization And Mapping.

Some key aspects are that the robot does not know where it is. It doesn't know if it is in the middle of the room, or in a corner, or wherever. It does not know what objects are in the room. It must navigate around, trying to figure out the room, doing so as it moves around. Unlike my example of being in the dark, we can allow the robot to have various sensory capabilities including vision, sonar, radar, LIDAR, and the like, and the room can be lit (there are various scenarios, some would be when the room is lit and the vision can see things, other circumstances might be when vision is not usable but other sensors are).

The robot is welcome to use its sensory devices as it so wishes to do so. We aren't going to put any constraints on the sensors that it has, though it only has whatever sensors have been provided. The conditions in the room might limit the efficacy of any given sensor at any given moment. If the room is dark, the vision sensor might not be providing much help. If the objects in the room tend to absorb sound waves, then it could be that the sonar won't do much good. And so on.

The robot must also have some kind of ability to move, which might be done by rollers rather than walking around the room. It doesn't matter much how it is able to move, but the crucial aspect is that it can and does move. By moving, it explores the environment. Without moving around, it would only be able to "see" whatever it can detect from its present location. By moving around, it will be able to go around and behind objects, and get a better sense of where things are in the room. Imagine if you were in a crowded room and had to stand stationary, and were asked to tell what else is in the room – it might be very hard to see over a large bookcase and know what is on the other side, without actually walking over to see.

What we want to do is have the robot be able to use its sensors, move around, ascertain the nature and shape of the room, and the nature and location of the objects in the room. Since it does not know where in the room it is, the robot must also figure out where it is. In other words, beyond just mapping what is around it, ultimately the robot needs to determine where it is. Figuring this out might not be very immediate. The robot might need to wander around for a while, and eventually after it has crafted a map of the environment, it could ascertain where it is in the environment.

Now that you hopefully comprehend the nature of the problem, I ask you to provide me with an algorithm that would be able to allow the robot to ultimately map out its environment and know where it is.

There are many that have tried to craft such an algorithm. SLAM is one of the most studied aspects of robotics, and particularly for autonomous vehicles. If we were to send an autonomous vehicle up to the planet Mars, we would want it to be able to do SLAM. On a more day-to-day basis, suppose we want to send a robot into a house where a gunman is holed-up. The robot needs to use SLAM to figure out the layout of the house and get to the gunman. You can imagine the look on the gunman's face when they see the robot navigating around the room. Think of this as an advanced version of Roomba, the popular robotic vacuum cleaner.

I suppose you are already drafting on a napkin the algorithm that you would devise for the SLAM problem. Well, I hate to tell you this, but it turns out there are lots of possible algorithms. The thing is, we don't want just any algorithm, we want one that is reasonably tractable in computational time and that can be presumably relatively efficient in what it does. If your algorithm would take computers twenty years nonstop to figure out the layout of the room, it probably is not an algorithm we would find very useful.

To deal with the computational aspects, we'll allow that the SLAM can be an approximator. This means that rather than seeking true perfection about the determined layout and locations, we'll be okay with the aspect that there will be probabilities involved. So, rather than my saying that I am standing at an exact latitude and longitude down to the millimeter, if you can say that I am likely within a specific square area within the room, it might be sufficient for purposes of being able to navigate throughout the room. We'll allow uncertainties for the sake of brevity and quickness.

Consider that with SLAM you are able to have some set of sensory observations, we'll call it O. These are collected sensory aspects that have happened at discrete time steps, we'll call it T. You are to create a map of the environment, we'll call it M, and be able to indicate the location of the robot, which we'll call X.

One of the more popular ways to solve this problem involves the use of Grid Maps. Imagine a large grid, consisting of cells, and into each cell we are going to mark some aspect about the environment, such as whether there is an object in that cell position of not. The grid becomes a kind of topological map of the environment. We can update the grid as the robot moves around, improving the grid indications of what it has found so far. Particular objects are considered to be landmarks. If we don't have any readily available landmarks, the problem becomes somewhat harder and we can only use raw data per se. The sensors are crucial since the less of them we have, and the less they each can detect aspects of the room, the less we have to go on for making the grid.

Here's some of the processing involved in SLAM:

Landmark detection and extraction

Data association with other found objects

State estimation of the robot

State update of the robot position

Landmark updates as we proceed

The simpler version of SLAM involves only considering 2D motion. Thus, this would be a robot confined to moving around on the ground and unable to jump up or fly. The harder version of SLAM involves dealing with 3D motion, such as a drone that can fly and so it has not only the 2D aspects but also the added third dimension too.

One of the most popular algorithms used in SLAM is the Extended Kalman Filter (EKF). It is a mathematical way to keep track of the uncertainties of the robot position and the uncertainties of the environmental layout of objects.

For much of the existing research on SLAM, there are some heavy constraints used. For example, one such constraint is that individual landmarks or objects much be distinguishable from each other. This prevents the robot from getting confused by thinking that object A is over here and over there, at the same time, when in actuality it is object A in location Q and it is object B over in location R. There is often a constraint that the landmarks or objects must be stationary and cannot move. Even in spite of these constraints, the algorithm must also be able to try and figure out if it has associated a landmark or object with the wrong thing, in other words it must try to prevent itself from confusing object A with object B.

A breakthrough in figuring out SLAM occurred when there was a realization that the correlations between various identified landmarks or objects was helpful rather than either unimportant or hurtful to the process. Many researchers trace this realization to a 1995 mobile robotics research paper that showed there was a convergence possible due to the use of the correlations.

For robots that are primarily using vision, there are variants of SLAM known as V-SLAM. The letter V stands for Visual. Along with this, there is Visual Odometry (VO). A robot might normally keep track of its odometry or position by the trajectory of its wheels and the distance traveled. Some instead prefer to use a camera that takes frames and a comparison between the frames helps determine the movement of the robot. There's an interesting article on the semantic segmentation-aided visual odometry for urban autonomous driving in the September-October 2017 issue of the Journal of Advanced Robotic Systems, which you should take a look at if you want to know more about VO and V-SLAM.

Which brings us to this — what does SLAM have to do with self-driving cars?

At the Cybernetic Self-Driving Car Institute, we are making use of SLAM to aid the AI of self-driving cars.

You might at first glance think that it is obvious that SLAM should be used for self-driving cars. Well, not exactly so.

Remember that SLAM is predicated on the notion that the robot does not know where it is and does not know the nature of the environment that it is in.

For most self-driving cars, they are normally going to have a GPS and IMU in order to figure out where they are positioned. They don't need to guess. They can use their instruments to find out where they are.

In terms of the driving environment, self-driving cars are going to usually have an extensive detailed map provided to them. For example, the Waymo self-driving cars in Arizona are being situated in a locale that has been mapped over and over by Google. The engineers have meticulously mapped out the streets and objects, doing so such that the self-driving car has the map already handed to it. They are also geo-fencing the self-driving cars, preventing the self-driving cars from going outside the boundaries of the already mapped surroundings.

Yikes! You are probably wondering why in the world I dragged you through this whole SLAM thing. If the self-driving car will already know its position, due to GPS and IMU, and if the self-driving car will know its environment in terms of layout and objects by an extensive pre-mapping effort, it would seem that SLAM has no purpose here. Case closed. No SLAM, none of the time.

Not so fast!

We are aiming to have true Level 5 self-driving cars. These are self-driving cars that can drive in whatever manner a human could drive. I ask you, does a human driver always know in-advance the surroundings of where the human driver is driving? No, of course they don't. Does the human driver always know where the car is? Not for sure, sometimes, such as when you get lost in a neighborhood that you've not driven in before.

Now, I realize that you could counter-argue that with GPS, there should never be a circumstance of a human driver that doesn't know where they are. This is somewhat true and somewhat untrue. Suppose the GPS goes down or is unavailable? I find that when I am in downtown San Francisco, for example, the GPS often loses signal and it does not know where I am on the map. This can be due to blockage of the GPS signals via tall buildings or for atmospheric reasons.

One might also say it is arguable that we will have all places mapped a priori. Admittedly, there is a lot of mapping taking place by Google and others. Furthermore, once self-driving cars become more prevalent, if they share their collected info then we'll gradually have more and more maps available by the collective will of all those self-driving cars.

But, still, there are going to be places where you'd like to go with your self-driving car and that are not yet mapped and that might not have reliable GPS. SLAM can come to rescue in those instances. And, where SLAM will likely especially be helpful is with autonomous bicycles. Yes, imagine a bicycle that does what a self-driving car does, but that it is a bicycle. A bicycle can go to a lot of places that a car cannot go. Bicycles can go through narrow spaces and go on roads that a car cannot go onto. A great exploration of the use of SLAM for bicycles is described in an article on simultaneous localization and mapping for autonomous bicycles that appeared in the May-June 2017 issue of the International Journal of Advanced Robotic Systems.

Simply put, any AI self-driving car developer should know about and be versed in SLAM.

Even if your specialty related to AI self-driving cars is some other aspect of the system, knowing the capabilities and limits of SLAM would be helpful to your endeavors. We will continue to need SLAM, and especially when self-driving cars try to go outside of carefully orchestrated geo-fenced populated areas. In some respects, a small town such as say the town of Pinole is about the same as driving on Mars. Once we get to Mars, I suppose we can just ask the Martians for directions, but in the meantime, lets continue pushing forward on SLAM.

CHAPTER 5

SWARM INTELLIGENCE FOR AI SELF-DRIVING CARS

CHAPTER 5

SWARM INTELLIGENCE
FOR AI SELF-DRIVING CARS

There was a dog on the freeway the other day.

I've seen a lot of items scattered on the freeways during my daily commute, including lawn chairs, ladders, pumpkins (a truck carrying Halloween pumpkins had gotten into an accident and spilled its load of pumpkin patch pumpkins), and whatever else can seem to drop onto, spill into, or wander along on the freeway. A live animal is always an especially big concern on the freeway. Besides the danger to the animal, there is also usually heightened danger to the freeway drivers. The likely erratic behavior of the animal can cause drivers to make mistakes and ram into other cars. Also, invariably some good Samaritans try to get out of their cars and corral the animal on the freeway. This puts those well intended humans into danger too from errant car drivers.

Anyway, in this case, I watched in amazement as my fellow drivers all seemed to work cooperatively with each other. Cars nearest tp the dog were careful to give it some distance so that it would not be scared into bolting further along on the freeway. Cars next to those cars were trying to run interference by moving into positions that would force other cars to go widely around the protected pocket. Cars at the outer layers had turned on their emergency flashers and were essentially directing other cars to flow into the outermost lanes. In the end, fortunately, the dog opted to run toward a freeway exit and was last

63

seen happily getting off the freeway and into a nearby neighborhood.

Let's review for a moment what happened in this case of the saved dog.

Did all of us drivers get onto our cell phones and talk with each other about what to do? Nope. Did an authority figure such as a policeman enter into the fray and direct us to provide a safe zone for the dog? Nope. So, in other words, we somehow miraculously all worked together, in spite of not directly speaking with each other, and nor by having someone coordinate our activities for us. We spontaneously were able to work as a group, even though we all had never met each other and we carried on no direct communication with each other per se.

Miracle? Well, maybe, maybe not. Have you ever watched a flock of birds? They seem to coordinate their movements and do so perhaps without having to directly communicate with each other. Same goes for a school of fish. Same goes for a colony of ants, bees, wasps, and those darned pesky termites. Generally, there are numerous examples in nature of how animals essentially self-organize themselves and exhibit collective aggregated behavior that provides a useful outcome for the group and provides benefits for the members of the group too. This collective behavior is typically characterized by a decentralized governance, meaning that there is not one centralized authority that directs the activities of the group, but instead the control of the group and the individuals is dispersed.

Swarm Intelligence (SI). That's what this kind of behavior is called, at least within the field of AI and robotics that's what we call it. If you prefer, you can call it swarm behavior. The swarm behaviorists are prone to studying how animals end-up being able to act as a flock, school, colony, or any other such grouping. Those of us studying swarm intelligence are more focused on getting technology to do the same kind of swarm behavior that we see occurring in animals. Some also don't like to say that swarm intelligence is appropriate for things like say termites, since they argue that termites are not "intelligent" and so it is better to simply refer to them as having swarm behavior. We could debate at some length whether termites are "intelligent" or at least have intelligent-like characteristics – I'm going to avoid that acrimonious debate herein and save it for another day.

Swarm intelligence is a pretty hot topic these days. There have been many that are working on individual robots and individual drones for a long time, trying to get AI to appear in those individualized things. There are others that want to leverage the individualized thing and have it do wonderous acts by coming together as a swarm. Imagine a swarm of a hundred drones and how they might be able to deliver packages to your door, either each flying your ordered new pair of pants or maybe they work together to carry a refrigerator to you (able to handle the weight of the refrigerator by having many drones each bearing some of the weight). You can also imagine the military applications for swarming, such as having an army of robots to fight battles.

One of the major questions in swarming is how much intelligence does the individual member of the swarm need to have. If you believe that ants are pretty ignorant, and yet they are able as a group to accomplish amazing feats, you would argue that members of a swarm don't need to have much intelligence at all. You could even say that if the swarm members have too much intelligence, they might not swarm so well. The self-thinking members might decide that they don't want to do the swarm. If instead they are rather non-intelligent and are just acting on instinct, they presumably won't question the swarm and will mindlessly go along with the swarm.

The swarm participants do need to coordinate in certain kinds of ways, regardless of how intelligent or not they each are. In the 1980's, there were studies done of birds in flocks, and a researcher named Craig Reynolds developed a computer-based simulation that involved bird-oid objects, meaning bird like simulations, and this came to be known as boids. Thus, you can refer to each individual member of a swarm as a boid. The birds in a flock are boids in that swarm, while the ants in a colony are the boids in that swarm.

In the boids simulation, there were three crucial rules about aspects of a swarm:

–   Separation

–   Alignment

–   Cohesion

In the case of separation, each boid needs to keep away from each other boid, just enough as a minimum that they don't collide with each other. A bird in a flock needs to stay far enough away from the birds next to it that they won't accidentally run into each other. This distance will depend on how fast they are moving in the swarm and how much the swam shifts in direction. The separation distance can vary at times during the swarm. The relative distance will also vary from type of boid such as fish versus birds versus ants. If the distance between the boids gets overly large, it can also impact the swarm, such as the swarm losing its formation and becoming more like a seemingly random and chaotic collection rather than a self-organized one. On the other hand, you can have biods that actually link physically with each other, such that there is no distance between them at all (this is considered an intentional act rather than an accidental collision of the boids).

In the case of alignment, each boid aligns with the other boids in order to proceed in some direction. There has been much study done about why flocks or colonies go in particular directions. It can be driven at times by sunlight, or by earth magnetism, or by veering away from predators, or by veering toward food, and so on. The key here is that they align individually in order to steer toward some direction. They collectively go in that direction. The direction is not usually static, in the notion that the direction will change over time. They might go in one direction for a long time and then suddenly shift to another direction, or they might continually be shifting their direction.

In the case of cohesion, this refers to the individuals having a collective center of mass. You might have some members that are not necessarily going in exactly the same direction as others, but they overall are all exhibiting cohesion in that they still remain together in a flock, colony, or whatever. You've likely seen birds that have joined in a flock and can see splintering factions that appear to nearly be wanting to go off on their own, but in the end they continue to go along with the rest of the flock. As such, this swarm would be said to have strong cohesion.

Overall, any given swarm will have either strong or weak separation, strong or weak alignment, and strong or weak cohesion. There are other factors involved in depicting and developing swarms, but these three factors of separation, alignment, and cohesion are especially at the core of swarm principles.

I will though add one other important factor to this swam discussion, namely stigmergy. Stigmergy is the aspect that embodies the self-organizing element of the swam. It presupposes that one action of the swarm leads to the next action of the swarm. The spontaneous coming together of the boids turns into an emergent systematic activity, and for each act there is a next act that follows. A flock of birds turns left and rises, which then leads to the birds turning to the right and going lower, which leads to the birds flying level and straight ahead. One action stimulates the performance of the next action.

Notice that there are some factors that aren't being mentioned and so by default are not encompassed by traditional swarms. There is no control of the entire swarm. There is no planning by the swarm. There is no direct communication among the members of the swarm. This is what makes swarms so interesting as a subject matter. We usually spend much of our time assuming that to get intelligent group behavior you must have direct communication between members of the group, they must have some form of centralized control, and they must have some form of planning. This would seem to be the case for our governmental bodies such as a congress or similar, and the same for companies and how they turn individual workers into a collective that involves direct communication, planning, and uses executive centralized control. Not so with swarms.

Remember my story about the dog on the freeway? In that story, I purposely pointed out that none of the drivers directly communicated with each other. We did not call each other on our cell phones. I purposely mentioned that the police had not shown up to direct us toward working together (thus, there was in this case no centralized control). We had not prearranged a plan of how to protect the dog. Instead, it all happened spontaneously.

We essentially acted as a swarm.

The cars all kept a distance from each other to avoid hitting each other (separation). We shaped ourselves to help protect the dog and force other traffic around the dog (alignment). We were all moving together, at a slow speed, and remained tied together in a virtual manner (cohesion). Maybe I should get a T-shirt that says "I was a boid today and saved a dog!"

What does swarms have to do with self-driving cars?

At the Cybernetic Self-Driving Car Institute, we are developing AI systems that make use of SI (Swarm Intelligence) for self-driving cars.

You've probably read or heard that one of the claimed great advantages of self-driving cars will be that there won't be anymore traffic tie-ups on the highways. Those proponents are saying that self-driving cars will collectively work together to ensure that we don't have bogged down bumper-to-bumper traffic like we do today. The claim is that human drivers of today are not able to adequately coordinate with each other and therefore the emergent group behavior is that we are stymied in traffic.

You've maybe seen that trucking companies are aiming towards having "fleets" of AI self-driving trucks that work in unison, acting as a coordinated convoy. Self-driving truck after self-driving truck will be aligned with each other, and a lead self-driving truck will guide them to where they need to go. It is almost like a train, involving self-driving trucks that are akin to railcars that hook together to form a long train, but rather than physically being connected these self-driving trucks will be virtually connected to each other.

There are going to be a number of issues around these kinds of arrangements.

One issue is the aspect of freewill.

If you are in a self-driving car, and it is being somehow coordinated as part of overall traffic on the freeway, will you have any say over what your self-driving car does? Those that are proponents of the self-driving car as a freeway clogging solution would tend to say that you won't have any freewill per se. Your self-driving car will become part of the collective for the time you are on the freeway. It will obey whatever it is commanded to do by the collective. They tell you that this is good for you, since you, an occupant but no longer a driver, won't need to worry about which lane to be in, nor how fast to go. This will all be done for you, somehow.

One wonders that if this is indeed to be the case, if this is our future, whether it even matters that the self-driving car has much if any AI capabilities. In other words, if the self-driving car is going to be an all-obedient order taker, why does the self-driving car need any AI at all? You could just have a car that basically is driven by some other aspect, like a centralized control mechanism. No need for the self-driving car to do much itself.

Some say that the self-driving car will have and needs to have robust AI, and that it will be communicating with other self-driving cars, using V2V (vehicle to vehicle communications) to achieve coordinated group behavior. Therefore, when your self-driving car is on the freeway, it will discuss the freeway conditions with other self-driving cars that are there, and they will agree to what should be done. Your self-driving car might say to another one, hey, let me pass you to the left in the fast lane. And the other self-driving car says, okay, that's seems good, go for it.

We don't though know how these self-driving car discussions are going to be refereed. Suppose that I am in a hurry, and so I want my self-driving car to get to work right away. I instruct my self-driving car to bully other self-driving cars. But, suppose all the other self-driving cars are also in the bullying mode. How will this work? We might end-up back into the same freeway snarls that we already have today. There are some that argue that we'll need to have a points system. When my self-driving car gets onto the freeway, maybe my self-driving cars says it is willing to give up 100 points in order to get ahead of the other self-driving cars. Those other self-driving cars then earn points by allowing my self-driving car to do this. They, in turn, at some later point, can use their earned points to get preferential treatment.

Now, all of this covers the situation wherein the self-driving cars are communicating with each other. They either directly communicate with each other, via the V2V, or maybe they are under some kind of centralized control. There is the V2I (vehicle to infrastructure), which involves cars communicating with the roadways, and some believe this will allow for centralized control of cars.

Suppose though that we say that the self-driving cars aren't going to directly communicate with each other. They might have that capability to do so, but lets say that they don't need to do so. We then are heading into the realm of the swarm.

We are working on swarm algorithms and software that allows AI self-driving cars to act together and yet do so without having to do any pre-planning, without having any centralized control, and without having do to direct communication with each other. The self-driving cars become the equivalent of boids. They are like birds in a flock, or ants in a colony, or schools of fish.

This makes sense as a means to gain collective value from having self-driving cars. This also does away with the requirement of the self-driving cars having to negotiate with each other, and also allows them "freewill" with respect to the driving task.

I'll toss into the mix a wrinkle that makes this harder than it might seem at first glance. It is easiest to envision a swarm of AI self-driving cars that act in unison based on emergent behaviors when you have exclusively AI self-driving cars. The problem becomes more difficult once you add human drivers into the swarm. I know that some have a utopian view that we are going to have all and only self-driving cars and that we'll ban the use of human drivers, but I'd say that's a long, long, long ways in the future (if ever).

For now, it is more realistic to realize that we are going to have self-driving cars that are driving in the same roadways as human drivers.

With our software for the self-driving cars, the self-driving cars will know how to become part of a swarm. The question will be how will human drivers impact the swarm. It is like having a school of fish in which some of the fish aren't necessarily of a mind to be part of the school. Now, that being said, when you look closely at a school of fish, you will see that other fish will at times enter into the swarm and either join it, disrupt it, or pass through it. We are assuming that human drivers will do likewise when encountering an AI self-driving car swarm.

What would have happened if self-driving cars had encountered a dog on the freeway? Right now, most of the auto makers and tech companies are programming the AI self-driving cars to pretty much come to a halt when they come upon a moving animal. There is no provision for the self-driving cars to act together to deal with the situation. We believe that robust self-driving cars should be able to act together, doing so without necessarily needing direct communication and without needing any centralized control. A swarm of AI self-driving cars that has swarm intelligence would have done the same that we humans did, forming an emergent behavior that sought to save the dog and avoid any car accidents in doing so. That's really good Swarm Intelligence to augment Artificial Intelligence (which, by the way, I do have a nifty T-shirt that says "I Love AI+SI!"

CHAPTER 6

BIOMIMICRY AND ROBOMIMICRY FOR AI SELF-DRIVING CARS

CHAPTER 6

BIOMIMICRY AND ROBOMIMICRY
FOR AI SELF-DRIVING CARS

The fish in the aquarium tank were going round and round the inner edges of the glass surface that encased them in water. Humans watching the fish were likely wondering whether or not the fish knew they were in water. There is an ongoing philosophical debate about whether or not fish can comprehend that they are immersed in water. Maybe they take it for granted just like we take for granted that we are surrounded by air. Maybe they are actually deep thinkers and know they are in water and that they must stay in water to survive. Or, maybe they have no capacity to think per se and so the question of whether they are in water is not even something that they can entertain.

Regardless of the broader question about whether fish know they are in water, the humans watching the fish were looking for something else. The humans were researchers that wanted to see if the fish would demonstrate certain kinds of behaviors. For you see, the experimenters had created a robotic version of a fish and were waiting eagerly to see if the regular fish would accept the robo-fish as one of their own. If the living fish swam along with the robo-fish, it would tend to imply that the real fish were not frightened or otherwise taken aback by the robo-fish.

Indeed, the fish were swimming right along with the robo-fish, all of them going round and round in the tank. Success for robo-fish!

The researchers were wondering too whether the robo-fish could even get the fish to change their behavior, somewhat, such as convincing the fish to follow the direction of the robo-fish. Up until now, the robo-fish had been swimming in the same direction as the fish. This seems to suggest that the fish had accepted that the robo-fish was safe to be near. Would they also though be willing to change their own behavior and end-up following the robo-fish. In some mild respects, yes, it turns out that the fish would follow-up along with the robo-fish. More success for robo-fish!

Now, don't go too far on this. It's not as though the robo-fish got the living fish to do the macarena macaroni dance in the middle of the water tank. Instead, it was more akin to slightly altering the direction they were already headed and so a very modest impact on their behavior. But, who knows, maybe one day we'll be creating robo-fish that are the king of the fishes. All fish hail to the robo-fish! It could become a takeover of all fish by the robots, which presumably (hopefully!) are being controlled by the humans. So, humans control the robo-fish, which in turn control the fish. I know this might seem quite untoward and maniacal. Maybe another version of the future is that robo-fish will live in harmony with regular fish, and they will all help each other. Robo-fish and regular fish will become blood brothers, though I guess without the blood part of it.

One of the research studies about robo-fish that caught my attention involves the study of zebrafish and the development of a modular robotic system that mimics this small fish's locomotion and body movements. The work is being done at the Robotic Systems Lab in the School of Engineering at the Ecole Polytechnique Federale de Lausanne in Switzerland, and with the Paris Interdisciplinary Energy Research Institute at the University Paris Diderot.

Let me point out that trying to create a robot that is as small as a zebrafish and that has the same motion pattern and look as a zebrafish is a hard problem. The system is known as the Fish Control Actuator Sensor Unit or Fish-CASU, and it attempts to not only look like a zebrafish but also aims to swim at the same linear speed and acceleration as the real fish. There are two main components, the

FishBot and the RiBot, and it uses the popular Raspberry Pi processor along with a computer that communicates via Bluetooth and infrared with the robo-fish.

By first carefully studying the zebrafish, the researchers were able to determine that the fish follow a particular sequence while moving in the tank. The first step involves the zebrafish gaining their orientation and they do caudal peduncle bending to start their propulsion. Next, the fish go into a high linear acceleration mode. Third, in the relaxation step, they stop their tail beating and begin to glide in the water, gradually their linear speed decreases during this step. Generally, the zebrafish then repeat those three steps, over and over. The researchers opted to develop a finite-state machine that would get the robo-fish to do roughly the same, namely the orientation, acceleration, and then relaxation steps.

The idea of building machines that mimic the behavior of animals is of course a notion that has been with us for a very long time. Biomimicry is the study and attempt at trying to mimic the behavior of biological creatures. If you look at the work of Leonardo da Vinci, you can see that he was fascinated by birds and hoped to someday develop a machine that would allow man to fly like birds do. Even the Wright Brothers likewise used biomimicry to help get mankind off the ground and flying into the air.

As they say, imitation is the highest form of flattery. If animals can do something, perhaps we can create machines to do the same.

One twist to this topic involves the aspect of potentially changing the behavior of the mimicked creature. In other words, it's one thing for us to be able to fly in airplanes, and another to have us use biomimicry inspired robots to change the behavior of the birds. Suppose we created a robo-eagle and had it fly along with eagles. Maybe the robo-eagle could warn real eagles when a hunter was trying to shoot at the eagles, or maybe keep the eagles from running into the wall of a building or into the engine of a jet plane. You could say that the biomimicry could be used for purposes of good, augmenting the true creatures and aiding them. As with anything that involves good, there's the chances too of the bad, such as maybe using the robo-eagle to lure the eagles into a trap of some kind and lead to their destruction or extinction.

Anyway, the overall point is that we can study living creatures and try to create robo-like versions of them and then use those robo-versions to possibly change the behaviors of the creatures themselves. The part in which we try to create robo-like versions is what I call biomimicry. The part about using the robo-like version to then change the behavior of the living creature I call robomimicry. In essence, the living thing begins to mimic the robot thing.

What does this have to do with AI self-driving cars?

At the Cybernetic Self-Driving Car Institute, we are using the techniques of biomimicry and robomimicry to understand and enhance the AI of self-driving cars. This will be important along the path toward achieving true self-driving cars, those that are at the level 5. A level 5 self-driving car is one that can drive the car in whatever manner a human could drive the car. To-date, we've seen mainly level 2 and level 3 self-driving cars, and some auto makers and tech firms are just getting to the edges of level 4. We still have a long ways to go before we get to a true level 5.

From a biomimicry perspective, you could say that we are already trying to mimic the biological creatures that underlie cars, namely the human drivers. I realize this seems a bit odd in that usually you think of biomimicry as trying to mimic perhaps a horse, or a bird, or fish. In the case of cars, cars are already a type of machine, but there is a biological component essential to that machine, which is the human that drives the machine. Therefore, it makes sense that we would want to mimic the human driver when trying to create a "robot" that can do the same thing (an AI self-driving car).

Allow me a moment to give an example of how biomimicry can be subtly but demonstrably applied.

Recently, the Nissan 2018 Rogue SL AWD was released. The car has a limited version of self-driving capabilities, including the ProPilot smart adaptive cruise control. As akin to similar systems on other auto makers cars, it allows the system to steer and drive the car while in a constrained highway driving situation. The human driver must still remain attentive to the driving task. The driver's hands are to remain on the steering wheel, and the system the prompts the driver to periodically nudge the steering wheel to prove that they (the human driver) presumably are still paying attention to the road. Similar kinds of adaptive cruise controls are found on the Tesla Autopilot, the Mercedes Benz DistronicPlus, and the Cadillac SuperCurise.

In the case of the ProPilot, it often appears to move back-and-forth within the lane. It veers toward the leftmost part of the lane, and then corrects itself toward the center, and then tends to veer toward the rightmost part of the lane. Many would not notice the car doing this. It takes a keen eye and an awareness of driving behaviors to readily realize this aspect. In some respects, this would be the same as a novice driver, imagine a student learning to drive. They over-correct in one direction and then the next. The ProPilot also tended to at times brake sharply in traffic, seemingly as though it was belated in recognizing that it was time to apply the brakes. The acceleration would do the same, at times jerking forward and rapidly accelerating when a more gradual increase in speed would do.

A human driver that is a novice might do all of those things. They would be over-correcting within a lane and tend to "weave" rather than be able to keep a steady center-lane approach. They would tend to brake suddenly rather than gradually. They would tend to accelerate rapidly rather than gradually. A more seasoned and experienced driver would be able to generally keep to the center of the lane. They would be able to gauge when to apply the brakes and do so without a sense of dramatics to it. They would be able to accelerate in a smooth manner that would not have the occupants in the car feel like they are in a rocket that is zooming into outer space.

This behavior of the ProPilot could be enhanced by using biomimicry of human drivers, particularly seasoned human drivers. The smoother version of driving is what the self-driving car should attempt to achieve. The odds are that the ProPilot was programmed to consider the angles and torque and other driving factors to mathematically calculate what to do. By also then seeing how human drivers drive, the self-driving capability can become more like human drivers. This is one of the advantages of using machine learning as part of the AI development for self-driving cars. Machine learning based on large data sets of human driving are able to "mimic" the human driving behavior, even if the system itself does not necessarily have any logical reason for it per se, and instead it uses often neural networks which mainly try to find a pattern and mimic to that pattern.

Improvements in AI self-driving cars will occur as the AI becomes more biomimetic of how humans drive.

There is an additional twist to this. Right now, the biomimicry is based on how humans drive today. But, keep in mind that once AI self-driving cars become more prevalent on the roadways, we are likely to see a change in the driving behavior of humans.

Say, what?

Yes, we will begin to see human drivers changing their behavior due to the behaviors of the AI self-driving cars. In a sense, we'll see robomimicry.

Let's first look at what is going to happen as AI self-driving cars become somewhat common place on our roadways.

Here's the human reaction:

- Awe
- Wide Berth
- Acceptance
- Treat Like Second-Class Citizen
- Begin to Ignore or Disdain

At first, human drivers in their cars will tend to look at the AI self-driving cars in awe. Look, there goes a self-driving car! Let's follow it to see what it goes. Oh my gosh, did you see it come up to that red light, it made a perfectly good stop at the red light. And so on.

Most of the human drivers will opt to give a wide berth to the self-driving car. It will be the same kind of reaction that seasoned human drivers give to novice drivers. When you see a human driven car that has a sign "Student Driver" you usually give that car a wide berth. You figure that the human driver might do something untoward and will likely be driving in a very timid way. So, you switch lanes to go around it, or you give it extra distance from your car. Human drivers will tend to do the same with the first round of AI self-driving cars.

Gradually, we'll begin to see acceptance of the self-driving cars. They will be gradually improving in their AI driving capabilities. Rather than giving them a wide berth, instead we'll see a lot of human drivers that have lost the awe aspect, and instead are irritated or frustrated at the self-driving cars. Why is that darned self-driving car going so slowly? Why is it waiting so long at the stop sign? Human drivers will begin to see the self-driving car as a kind of second-class citizen.

We'll begin to see human drivers trying to trick or exploit the AI of the self-driving car.

Imagine these kinds of human driving behavior:

I know that the self-driving car waits a long time to make a right on a red light, so I'll swing around the self-driving car and sneak in front of it, allowing me (as a human) to make the turn without having to wait for the AI self-driving car to do so.

I'll outrace the self-driving car since I am willing to zip through a yellow light while the self-driving cars are all being cautious and coming to a halt as soon as they see the yellow light and don't want to race through an intersection.

Up ahead there is a self-driving car, and I can use it to block traffic for me, by getting in front of it, it will try to maintain the proper driving distance and I can then exploit it to prevent traffic from catching up with me.

These are examples of how human driving behavior will change, due to the introduction of AI self-driving cars. Those examples tend toward workarounds regarding the AI self-driving cars. We might say that those human driving behavior changes are "bad" because they are tending toward worse driving behavior by the humans.

Oddly enough, there is a chance that the changes in human driving behavior will be for the good. The robomimicry of human drivers mimicking the self-driving cars could actually get human drivers to be better drivers. If the AI self-driving cars are all tending toward the proper driving distances on the highways, it might get the human drivers to do likewise. If the AI self-driving cars exhibit minimal lane changes and it leads to faster traffic flow, perhaps human drivers will do the same. Whether the human drivers will do this because they mentally see the connection between how the AI self-driving cars are driving and their own driving behavior is an open question. It could be that the human drivers will just witness what is going on and tend to follow along, rather than overtly opting to drive differently.

Not all human drivers will be driving the same way. Some human drivers will more quickly adapt to the AI self-driving cars, while others will take longer to do so. Some human drivers will try to exploit the AI self-driving cars, while others won't. It will be a mix. Overall though, we need to realize that the introduction of AI self-driving cars onto the roadways will have an impact on human drivers. Currently, most researchers and auto makers are assuming people will drive as they do. It is assumed that the driving behavior of humans is static. The reality is that human driving behavior is dynamic. Humans will change as they see other facets of the roadways and how AI self-driving cars are driving. Biomimicry leads to robomimicry, which will lead to more biomimicry, and so on.

What will human drivers think of AI self-driving cars that eventually can drive as well and perhaps even better than humans? It reminds me of this famous quote by Immanuel Kant: "Even a man's exact imitation of the song of the nightingale displeases us when we discover that it is a mimicry, and not the nightingale."

CHAPTER 7

DEEP COMPRESSION
AND PRUNING
FOR AI SELF-DRIVING CARS

Dr. Lance Eliot and Michael B. Eliot

84

CHAPTER 7

DEEP COMPRESSION AND PRUNING FOR AI SELF-DRIVING CARS

When my son was very young, he and I played a board game that he seemed specially to enjoy. It required concentration and dexterity, and a bit of imagination along with a dose of excitement. If you made a mistake during the game, there would be a directly adverse reaction by the game. In some cases, if your action was really a lousy choice during the game, there would be a substantial clatter and reaction. Naturally, he didn't like losing the game and so tended to enjoy it more when others made a blunder rather than he. I recall that when I picked the wrong piece and caused the rest of the pieces to nearly "explode" upward, he would jump for joy. It's that competitive spirit in our DNA, I'm sure.

You might be familiar with the board game, called Booby Trap, which was quite popular in the 1960s when it first came out and still today can be found in most toy stores. The game involves placing various wood pegs into a bounded area of a small wooden platform and then using a spring-loaded bar to push together the pegs.

Essentially, the pegs are crammed together once the spring-loaded bar is put in place and the pegs are so sandwiched that they can be hard to pull out of the platform. And that's indeed the notion underlying the game, namely that you take turns with other players in trying to pull out pegs from the platform. If you can pull out a peg without having the spring bar move, or at least not move more than a stated distance, you earn points based on the designated value of that peg. The larger pegs are worth more points, of course, since they are more likely when extracted to potentially cause the spring-loaded bar to shift.

From a cognition and growth perspective, I played the game with my son and also my daughter as not only a means to have fun, but also since I figured it would be a good learning tool for them. One aspect of learning in this particular game is the effects of compression. When you compress items together, you need to think about how the physics of compression impacts other objects. In some instances, the compression would bear upon a handful of the pegs and the other pegs were not under any pressure at all. This at first was counter intuitive to my children as they initially assumed that applying pressure would cause all of the pegs to be under pressure. They mentally caught on and were then able to quickly determine which of the pegs weren't under pressure, and would lift those out when their turn during the game play occurred, thus avoiding the risk of having the spring-loaded bar move.

They also learned about the act of pruning. Removal of each of the pegs is essentially a type of pruning action. You are lessening the number of objects involved in the game play. The more you did of pruning, the harder the game play became, due to the aspect that you now had less pieces that were in a confined area and that were the only ones left holding the spring-loaded bar in place. If you went too far in your pruning, the spring-loaded bar would shift and you'd lose points. It took both a delicate hand and a sharp mind to be able to play this game.

Why care about this game? Well, it's a great introduction to some of the most important core elements of computer science. When storing data, you tend to not have unlimited storage space and therefore need to be thinking about how you can reduce the amount of data and yet still keep intact the meaning that the data represents. If you prune out the data overly so, you might have reduced the volume of data but at the same time you might have tossed out essential aspects and the loss is a bad thing. Likewise, you can try to keep the data around and rather than pruning it you might compress it. Compression compacts things together and can reduce the total amount of space, but at the same time you need to consider how readily you can get access to the data since it will require decompression to put it back into a readable state.

As an aside, I realize that some of you might be thinking that I was maybe a bit too serious with my children while playing games. I assure you that we played games for sport and fun! All I am saying is that the games themselves also provided handy lessons in life. Why not leverage those handy lessons and either consider that they will occur subliminally, and the child won't even realize what is taking place, or perhaps instead try to explicitly get the proverbial one-bird-with-two-stones. You can have your child play a game for both fun and for gaining new knowledge and lessons in life.

Anyway, let's get back to compression and pruning. Sometimes you only focus on pruning. Sometimes you only focus on compression. Sometimes it is handy to do both compression and pruning. From a computer viewpoint, the act of compressing and pruning can be computationally intensive and so you need to decide whether there is a valid Return on Investment (ROI) for doing so. If the effort to compress and prune is one-time, and then the result is used over and over, the cost to do the one-time upfront compressing and the pruning is more likely to be worthwhile. You are potentially able to reduce the amount of storage required overall and the compactness might allow for the data to be more easily and less expensively stored.

What does this have to do with AI self-driving cars?

At the Cybernetic Self-Driving Car Institute, we are using deep compression and pruning for machine learning to be able to have neural networks that are more compact and usable in self-driving cars.

The pruning of neural networks goes back to some of the earlier days of the advent of artificial neural networks. Numerous studies during the 1990s attempted to find ways to prune neural networks. The overarching idea is to consider all possible neural network topologies that apply to the problem at hand, and choose from these variants the one that has the same output at the smallest size. Unfortunately, trying to go through all possibilities to find the "best" one is generally infeasible due to the vast number of combinations and permutations that would need to be examined. As such, there are various pruning rules-of-thumb that have been developed that guide toward doing a less comprehensive pruning and yet also aim at trying to find a smaller sized neural network, even if it isn't the optimal smallest it is at least smaller than it might otherwise have been.

When developing a neural network, there are four major stages:

- Design of the neural network based on needs

- Training of the neural network to find a fit

- Completion of the neural network for ongoing use

- Fielding the neural network for real-world action

At the first stage, doing design, the developer needs to consider aspects such as how many layers to have, how many neurons to have, how many synapses (connections) to have, and so on. The outermost layers are usually devoted to receiving input and providing output, and thus are for primarily externality purposes. The other layers within the neural network are sometimes called hidden layers and are in-between the outermost layers. The neurons within each layer are interconnected among other neurons in that layer, and also can be interconnected to neurons in other layers. Each neuron can have some number of fan-in connections and some number of fan-out connections.

For a given problem that you are wanting to use a neural network for, you need to be considerate about how many layers, how many neurons, how many connections, etc. If you go hog-wild and just pick some arbitrarily large sizes, you'll likely find that the training effort can be quite high. If you go too conservative and don't have enough size, you'll be less likely to have the neural network be successful at trying to match to the problem and achieve the desired results.

Let's suppose that you are devising a neural network for trying to identify street signs. This neural network will be part of the AI self-driving car system. You want the neural network to be able to accurately find street signs when an image is presented to the neural network. The self-driving car has cameras that will be taking pictures and sending those to the on-board neural network. The neural network then tries to ascertain whether there is say a Stop sign ahead, and alerts the rest of the AI system so that the self-driving car will appropriately come to a stop.

The on-board neural network will consume storage space and processor time in order to do its thing of analyzing images that come from the self-driving car cameras. The computers on-board of the self-driving car need to be powerful enough to be able to house the neural network and fast enough to ensure that the neural network will do its matching in time. If the camera provides an image of a street sign, and if the self-driving car is moving ahead at a fast speed, and if it takes the neural network too long to figure out if the sign is a Stop sign, the AI of the self-driving car might run right through the Stop sign because of the lateness of getting the street sign analysis results from the neural network.

Consider that self-driving cars need tons upon tons of neural networks for analyzing all kinds of input coming from the cameras and the LIDAR and the sonar, etc., and you begin to realize that the amount of computers needed on-board and their storage needs is rather daunting. Plus, consider too the energy requirements for all of these computers. You'll need to have an enormous battery or other energy producing elements of the self-driving car just to power all of the computers needed on-board.

Thus, overall, it would be vital to try and keep the size of the neural networks to the least size feasible. This though must be done in a fashion that does not overly limit how well they work. If we were to prune and compress a street sign neural network so that it was tiny, but if it then did a lousy job of recognizing street signs, and suppose it could only figure out a Stop sign some of the time, we are then putting at heightened risk the rest of the self-driving car and the occupants too.

So, the developer during the design stage must try to gauge what size they think makes sense to use. Then, during the training stage, they have the neural network train on large samples of data and see how well the neural network can train onto the data. You want the neural network to reach a state of generalizability such that it will be able to work well once it is put into use. If the neural network "overfits" to the training data, it means that the neural network does well on the training set but that it will likely not do so well once it is put into use (due to becoming focused solely on the training data overly so).

After the neural network has been sufficiently trained, the developer then does some final completion aspects to get it ready for use on an ongoing basis. In some cases, the neural network will be sparse such as having swaths of neurons that are not used or connections that are not used, and so on. Most developers tend to think about pruning once they get to this completion stage of the effort. They might not realize that they already were likely doing pruning when they were in the design stage, in the sense that perhaps they initially setup the neural network at some size N that they could have done at size N+1, but instead opted to go with N. In other words, they did pruning simply by deciding at the outset what the size would be as they went into the training stage.

The point here is that you can do pruning at any of the stages. You can essentially do pruning when initially designing the neural network. Once the neural network is undergoing training, you can do pruning to see how it impacts the training. And, once the neural network is trained, during the completion stage you can do pruning. You can also do pruning once the neural network is fielded.

The types of pruning include:

- Prune the number of layers (this is usually the biggest bang for the buck)

- Prune the number of connections

- Prune the number of neurons

- Prune the number of weights

- Prune other aspects

If you can somehow eliminate an entire layer of the neural network then it often is the biggest bang for the buck in terms of reducing the size and complexity of the neural network. That being said, it is usually less likely that you can reduce an entire layer. Also, I don't want to mislead in that you could have a layer that is rather skimpy to begin with, and so the amount of pruning by eliminating that layer might not be as big a payoff as if you were able to prune the number of connections, or neurons, etc. Each neural network will have its own shape and so the pruning payoff depends upon that shape.

You should also be careful about assuming that pruning is easy.

Have you ever tried to prune a tree or a bush that maybe has become overgrown around your house? Just chop away it, you at first think. If you do so, you'll find that sometimes the tree or bush becomes so harmed that it won't grow back. There are at times right ways and wrong ways to do pruning. This is the case too with the neural network. If you prune in the wrong ways, you'll begin to lose the point of having the neural network at all. As such, during pruning, you need to examine how sensitive the neural network is to each of the pruning actions that you undertake.

Besides pruning, a developer should also consider how to possibly compress the neural network. For example, if you take a look at the weights used for the neurons, you can sometimes find that there are some weights that are zero (in which case those neurons are candidates possible for pruning), or that are near to zero (more candidates for pruning), or that are of a commonly repeated value that you could potentially compress them. One of the most popular compression techniques used for neural network compression is to apply Huffman coding. Essentially, the Huffman coding technique takes codes that appear frequently, such as the same weights being used over and over in the neural network, and produces an alternative code which is shorter in size, and yet will still return back the original code when needed (this is known as lossless data compression).

A handy research study on deep compression and pruning was recently done by researchers Song Han (Stanford University), Huizi Mao (Tsinghua University, Beijing), and William Dally (Stanford University), entitled "Deep Compression: Compressing Deep Neural Networks with Pruning, Trained Quantization, and Huffman Coding," and provided some impressive indications of how you can potentially dramatically reduce the size of a neural network if you invoke appropriate pruning and compression approaches. One must be cautious though about how much a pruning effort or compression effort will payoff since, as mentioned already, the nature and shape of the neural network will impact whether you have a strong payoff or a weaker payoff.

In the case of AI self-driving cars, the pruning and compression is most likely to have a strong payoff for a type of neural network known as convolutional neural network, which is a type of neural network used for image analysis and visual pattern matching. We've seen this work well on neural networks for street sign analysis in AI self-driving cars, and also for pedestrian detection neural networks too.

For many of the AI self-driving car developers, they are primarily right now trying to make neural networks that work for the AI self-driving car, and not as concerned about whether the neural networks take up a lot of storage or consume a lot of processing time. This will become more apparent to those developers once their neural networks are working in-the-field.

It is a big jump to go from a neural network that works well in the lab or in a simulation, and instead to have it work in the real world. Optimization will be key to machine learning being viable while on-board an AI self-driving car. We don't want to have neural networks that are like a Booby Trap waiting to spring at the worst of times while a self-driving car is zooming down the freeway at 70 miles per hour. Prune and compress, that's the lesson learned here.

CHAPTER 8
EXTRA-SCENERY PERCEPTION FOR AI SELF-DRIVING CARS

CHAPTER 8

EXTRA-SCENERY PERCEPTION FOR AI SELF-DRIVING CARS

I was driving on a highway in Northern California recently when I saw up ahead of me a wind turbine off the side of the road. I've seen modern wind turbines before, but this one caught my eye. I liked the design of it and this one was cranking pretty fast, hopefully generating lots of electrical power. As I got closer to it, I realized that there were quite a number of them, all lined up across a vast valley. In fact, as I got even closer, I could see hundreds of them, maybe even more. It was an amazing sight to see. Wind turbine upon wind turbine, nearly as far as the eye could see. Some were turning rapidly in the prevailing wind. Some were moving slowly. Others were standing still. I suppose I should have been paying attention to the highway, but I admit that I was in visual awe of this enormous collection of wind turbines.

I wondered who put all those wind turbines there. Why are they there, in terms of presumably this must be a very windy place? How much power do they generate? How long have the turbines been there? Is there a tour that one can take to see the wind turbines up close? How much maintenance do the wind turbines require? Do birds get whacked by the wind turbines? How do they protect wildlife from getting hurt? These and a zillion more questions entered into my mind.

In today's modern world, I could take a look at my GPS, let's assume that I was using Google, and find out where I was. I could then likely have done a search to find out more about the place. Turns out, I did indeed do so, and I discovered that I had just driven through Altamont Pass. It houses the Altamont Pass Wind Farm, one of the

95

first wind farms in the United States and considered one of the largest wind farms in the world. There are nearly 5,000 wind turbines there. The combined effort of the wind turbines produces nearly 600 megawatts of power. Amazing stuff!

What does this have to do with self-driving cars?

At the Cybernetic Self-Driving Car Institute, we are developing AI for self-driving cars that looks at the scenery around the self-driving car and will try to determine what is there. I realize that most self-driving cars are already doing this on a limited distance basis, namely that most self-driving cars are detecting nearby road signs, fire hydrants, sidewalks, walls, and the like. But, very few if any are looking beyond the immediate scenery.

In fact, we call this kind of AI the catchy phrase of Extra-Scenery Perception (ESP2). It is "extra" in that it looks outside the norm of what most self-driving cars are scanning. It tries to "perceive" the surrounding area of the self-driving car, doing so at a distance of the self-driving car such as a football field length away or more.

Of course, there is the conventional ESP, Extra Sensory Perception, and we are here admittedly playing a bit of humor on that wording, thus, we call ours ESP2, appending the number two, in order to distinguish it from the true use of the acronym ESP. We aren't yet reading people's minds with the AI of self-driving cars, though, as I've mentioned many times, we are working on BMI (Brain Machine Interfaces) for self-driving cars.

What would the ESP2 do for us? It would have detected the wind turbines and potentially let the occupant of the self-driving car know about the wind turbines. Besides detecting the wind turbines, it would have looked up information about them, and been able to tell the occupant the various facts that I've told you earlier in this article. Presumably, it could even have asked the occupant whether they would like to stop and take a tour, and possibly have connected with the online tour system of the wind farm and made sure that there were tickets available.

That's an example of how the ESP2 could be beneficial to the occupants of the car, doing so on a somewhat touristy kind of approach. There are though more serious kinds of aspects to developing the ESP2. Allow me a moment to share an example.

While I was driving past that wind farm, I also happened to notice that there were some tractors moving slowly on a dirt road that was adjacent to the wind farm. The busy tractors were a couple of miles up ahead of me and I could see that they were kicking up a lot of dirt. A large dust cloud was being created by the tractors. So what, you might ask? Well, I realized that eventually that dust cloud was going to be carried by the wind onto the highway. And, the timing looked like I might end-up driving right into that thick dust cloud. It wasn't covering the highway just yet, but by the pace of the wind it was a reasonable prediction to anticipate that the dust would arrive to the highway at about the same time that I passed nearby to the tractors.

For most AI and self-driving cars, the sensors are narrowly focused to a short distance from the car. As such, they would not have realized that the dust cloud was forming. Only once the self-driving car pretty much entered into the dust cloud would the sensors realize that something was amiss. By then, the cameras of the self-driving car might be so covered with dust that they no longer would work properly to gauge the visuals needed to properly drive the self-driving car.

If the AI had Extra-Scenery Perception, it would have been able to predict the possibility of the dust cloud. As such, the AI could then either decide to route the vehicle a different way, trying to avoid the dust cloud. Or, the AI could have opted to slow down the self-driving car and try to pace the self-driving car such that the dust cloud would float over the highway prior to arrival of the self-driving car, and be gone by the time the self-driving car reached that point of the roadway. Or, the AI could have decided that it would keep going, but then be prepared that the visual cameras of the self-driving car will become occluded. It could have even used special shutters over the cameras to protect them from the dust, being willing to have its eyes shut momentarily to ensure they did not get permanently damaged.

None of those anticipatory acts could be planned for, if the AI was not looking beyond the immediate scenery. Thus, the value of having Extra-Scenery Perception, if you will.

Currently, sadly, we aren't arming most of the self-driving cars with sensory devices that can look that far ahead. Also, there is so much effort going into just keeping the self-driving car on the road and not hitting obstacles, the idea of doing a larger scenery analysis is at the back of the bus, so to speak. It's a nice idea, some developers say, but they have bigger fish to fry right now. For us, the desire to get to a Level 5 self-driving car, which is one that can do anything a human driver could do, causes us to believe that it is important to be working on ESP2.

When you consider the nature of the Extra-Scenery Perception, you'd realize that there are two major kinds of aspects that it will be looking for: (1) enduring, and (2) emerging.

One aspect consists of things that are of an enduring nature. For example, the wind turbines are an enduring item. They are there now and will likely be there a week from now. The AI and ESP2 can build up a library of enduring items over time. Obviously, many of those items can be researched online too, such that via GPS you can have the AI figure out what you will be expecting to see up ahead. The description though of something such as a wind farm is not as precise as what you actually see when you drive nearby the item. Therefore, though the online research will be fruitful, there is nonetheless still a need to collect the local data about the enduring item as you drive past it.

With the advent of V2V (vehicle to vehicle) communications, we'll eventually be able to have each self-driving car inform another self-driving car about what is up ahead. Suppose that someone else that had been a few miles ahead of me had the ESP2 on their self-driving car, it could have detected the wind farm prior to my being able to see it, and have passed along to my self-driving car that the wind farm was coming up.

What would have been even more helpful likely would be the passing along of information about an emerging item. For example, the dust cloud was an emerging item. It was not of an enduring nature, and instead was something of a momentary or temporary nature. It's detection in real-time was essential as its impact was also in real-time. Emerging items are aspects that can have a more immediate impact on the self-driving car at the time of detection.

That's not to say that an enduring item might not also have an emerging aspect too. Suppose that one of the blades on a wind turbine suddenly broke off and went flying into the air. This is an emerging aspect that it would be handy for the AI to detect, and therefore take evasive action for the self-driving car if needed to avoid the flying blade.

This is an important point because you might think that an enduring item only needs to be scanned once. In other words, if I drove past the wind farm again, you might say there's no need to do a detection and analysis because I had already driven past it previously. That's not though taking into account that things change over time. We need to assume that even the enduring items will change over time. The second time analysis will be faster to undertake, since the AI mainly needs to ascertain only differences between what it determined before and what it determines now.

We are using Machine Learning (ML) as an essential element of the ESP2. For example, driving around farm areas it becomes apparent that there are likely chances of dust clouds. The ML portion tries to look for patterns of the extra-scenery objects and learn over time what they might mean for the efficacy of the self-driving car. This also would be placed into a shared database so that other self-driving cars could tap into it. Your individual self-driving car can benefit from the hundreds or ultimately thousands upon thousands of other self-driving cars that are doing EPS2 too.

One question that I get asked when I describe the Extra-Scenery Perception is whether it makes sense to be detecting and analyzing everything. If the AI is trying to analyze everything around it, this would seem to be a rather large problem, involving lots of processing time and lots of memory. Shouldn't instead the ESP2 only be invoked when needed?

That's the classic chicken-and-the-egg kind of question. How will the AI know when it is appropriate to invoke the ESP2? If it was not invoking it when the tractors were kicking up dust, there would have been no way to learn from the dust cloud. If it was not invoking it when the wind farm appeared, it would not have learned about the wind farm aspects. You could argue that the human occupant inside the self-driving car should tell the AI to start doing an analysis, such as maybe when I was looking out the window of the car that I could have told the AI of the self-driving car to pay attention to the dust cloud or pay attention to the wind farm.

Our view right now is that we're having the ESP2 working all the time. We figure that it is like a child that once it learns enough, the effort to be scanning all the time will be greatly reduced. We'd rather that it learns as much as it can, now, rather than waiting until some random moment when it needs to be urged into action by a human occupant.

This does bring up the interactivity with the human occupants. To some degree, the ESP2 could be considered like a tour guide that is advising the occupants. It also has the safety factor in mind, such as the dust cloud issue earlier described. The degree of chattiness would depend upon the desires of the human occupant. In any case, the Extra-Scenery Perception is more than just an idle add-on, since there are lots of circumstances wherein a faraway aspect can potentially endanger the self-driving car, and the sooner that the self-driving car realizes that the threat exists, the more options the AI has to try and prevent harm to the self-driving car and the human occupants.

CHAPTER 9

INVASIVE CURVE
AND
AI SELF-DRIVING CARS

CHAPTER 9

INVASIVE CURVE
AND
AI SELF-DRIVING CARS

The puff adder, a venomous snake, became an invading species in Florida after it was imported into the state as a pet but then was let loose into the local native environment. The Asian long horned beetle was inadvertently brought into the United States when it hitchhiked on imported agricultural products, and now is destroying forests in the northeastern parts of the U.S. The Giant African Land Snail (GALS) loves to eat plants and was inadvertently brought into Florida where it began to threaten the agricultural well being of the state.

We are under siege!

Plants and animals that are not native to the United States are often introduced into the United States and then are able to go on an invasive torrent. At times the invaders are intentionally brought in, such as the puff adder that some thought would be a great pet, while in other cases the invader sneaks in, such as the Asian long horned beetle that hitched a ride to here via imported agricultural products. Our efforts as humans has allowed for new alien species to find an ecological environment that allows them to flourish.

In some cases, we even help the alien species. We might transport the alien species across the country and allow it to readily get started into new neighborhoods. We become the dispersal agent. Whether it is an animal or plant that we carry in our planes, trains, boats, or via other means, we aid something that otherwise could not go large distances on its own, and we put it into new areas for potential invasion. Our awareness that an alien species is taking hold will at times vary from knowing what we are doing and at other times we are quite unaware of what we are doing.

If we begin to realize that we've allowed an alien species to gain new ground, there are some occasions where we might welcome the invasion, and other occasions wherein we want to stop it. Our cultural perceptions will partially determine whether we want the alien to continue or we want it to be curtailed. One moment, we might be promoting the alien invader and urging all to adopt it, while later on we might decide that the invader is harmful and decide that it needs to be eradicated. Depopulation of an alien species can be very difficult to undertake and requires various invasive barriers and trickery to slow down or remove.

Some invaders are able to leverage aspects of their new environment to then achieve high abundances rapidly. There might not be any native predators that help keep the invader volume pruned. There might not be any environmental conditions of their original origins that are equaled in the new region, such as a creature that normally cannot survive harsh cold weather, which then becomes unabated in a year-round warm weather climate in a newly implanted region. In fact, there is the enemy release hypothesis that postulates an invader can profit mightily by the avoidance of its otherwise natural enemies when those enemies are not present in a new environment. Humans have even sometimes opted to try and stop an invader by then bringing in a second invader, one that is a natural enemy of the first invader, in hopes of expunging the first invader (and then dealing with the second invader in some other fashion).

Generally, there are three major steps involved in the invasion process:

- Humans introduce the invader into a new environment

- Invader spreads in the new environment

- Invader integrates into the new environment

Of course, it is not always the case that humans are the ones that introduce the invader. It could be that an invader is brought into the United States by the winds and carried across our lands. Or, the invader might arrive by the sea. Overall, though, today's invaders are most likely being introduced by us humans.

I'll also point out that though I am focusing on invaders that come into the United States, it is the same kind of invading dynamics that occur for other countries. In other words, a natural plant or animal in the United States can be carried into another country and be considered an invader in that country. Don't want you to think that I am being myopic and considering that only the United States as somehow the land of invasions. It can happen anywhere.

There's also another interesting twist to invasion dynamics, namely the possibility of an invasion meltdown. Imagine that an invasive species known as X has established itself into a new ecosystem called A. The invasive species X is a strong invader and takes hold quite firmly in the ecosystem A. This X begins to overtake native species Y and Z.

Without the native species Y and Z, another invader Q that otherwise would not have had a chance at establishing itself in the new ecosystem, suddenly begins to flourish. Essentially, the original invader X has produced a sequence of changes that creates an invasion meltdown, and allows invaders to flow into the new ecosystem. It could be a cascade that becomes nearly impossible to stop as it reaches a widespread pervasive invasion level.

On the topic of invaders, I'd like to share with you the below numbers. This shows the year and a numeric count. I won't say just yet what the count represents, and will keep you in suspense until later in this discussion:

1900:   8,000

1910:   458,000

1920:   8,132,000

1930:   23,035,000

1940:   27,466,000

1950:   40,339,000

1960:   61,671,000

1970:   89,224,000

1980: 121,601,000

1990: 133,700,000

2000: 225,821,000

2010: 250,070,000

I'll let you think about what those counts might be. It seems obvious that the counts are going up. And, there has been a rapid rise, especially at the start, going from a count of 8,000 to a count of 458,000 in just the first ten years of introduction. Over a one hundred and ten years span, the count went from the lowly starting point of 8,000 to become more recently a massive count of 250,070,000. Seems like a pretty successful "invader" upon quick glance.

So, what does all this talk about invasive species have to do with AI self-driving cars?

At the Cybernetic Self-Driving Car Institute, besides developing AI systems for self-driving cars, we also examine the socioeconomic aspects of the emergence of self-driving cars. As such, and this might seem surprising or even shocking to you, we assert that the adoption of self-driving cars could be considered an invasive dynamic.

Yes, it could be that once self-driving cars are introduced into our environment, we might begin to see a phenomenon similar to what happens when an invasive species is introduced into a new environment.

Right now, we have around 260 million conventional non-self-driving cars in the United States. The estimated number of AI self-driving cars in the United States today is tiny in comparison. In fact, none of the AI self-driving cars are yet at the true Level 5 of self-driving cars (which is the point at which self-driving cars are driven by AI as though it was the same as if a human driver was driving the car). Currently, there are a smattering of maybe Level 4 self-driving cars, mainly being used experimentally, and otherwise the rest of the self-driving cars are somewhere between a Level 2 and a Level 3.

As such, the invasion of the true AI self-driving car has not actually yet begun. But, we believe a true Level 5 self-driving car is possible and that we will ultimately have such cars on our roads, and thus, one could construe the eventual emergence of the true self-driving car as a kind of invader. Presumably, the self-driving car will begin to edge out the non-self-driving car. Some utopian believers seem to think that overnight we'll all switch from non-self-driving cars to self-driving cars, but realistically it will take a long time for such a switchover to occur. The economic cost to switch cars from today's pervasive non-self-driving cars to the emerging self-driving cars will prohibit a magical overnight transformation.

Remember when earlier I had stated that humans are the ones that tend to introduce an invading species, well, that's certainly going to be the case with the true AI self-driving cars. We, the humans, will be introducing the self-driving invader into our ecosystem. I know this kind of sounds like crazy talk, in that an AI self-driving car is not an invading plant or animal, and so you might be wondering how can we think of an inanimate object as an invading species.

Some would argue that the AI elements of the true self-driving car make it closer to a living organism than if we were referring to say refrigerators as invaders or toothbrushes as invaders. They would also point out that the self-driving cars will have the potential for life and death over us humans, while a toothbrush or refrigerator does not have that same significance.

I don't think we even need to get into the argument about whether the AI self-driving car is somehow sentient and whether or not we need to consider it as a kind of living thing. Put aside for the moment that whole debate. We can simply consider that we are going to see an introduction of something new into our existing transportation ecosystem, and that the new thing is a self-driving car. From that perspective, we can still make use of the invader dynamics as a framework for considering how this "new species" will take hold.

Indeed, you can consider that there are two viewpoints on the adoption of the true self-driving cars, either you think it is a good thing and we should definitely do it, or you think it is a bad thing and we should consider it a pest that needs to be stopped.

Right now, it seems like the mass media wants us to think that the true self-driving car is a good thing and so it is a welcomed invader that we want to encourage. The basis for this belief is the claim that a true self-driving car won't get drunk, it won't get tired, and otherwise will drive a car much better and more safely than humans do. That's certainly the hope, but we don't yet know that's going to be the case. I am sure that you might say that well, if the true self-driving cars aren't as good or better than human drivers then we just won't allow them to proceed, or at least we'll limit how far they can proceed and until they are perfected. If you are saying this, I think you have just fallen into the whole point about thinking of the true self-driving car as a potential invader. As mentioned earlier, sometimes humans first believe that an invader is a good thing, and later on change our minds and decide it isn't a good thing. We then either want to stop it, or maybe at least limit how much it takes hold.

Let me for a moment return to my earlier listing of years and counts. You might still be trying to determine what those counts represent (I gave you a subtle clue when I said that there are about 260 million conventional cars in the United States today). As indicated, the counts over a one hundred and ten years span went from the starting point of 8,000 to become more recently a count of 250,070,000. If you guessed that it was the introduction of the automobile in the United States, you'd be right! These are figures reported by various United States governmental bodies that keep track of the number of registered automobiles in the United States.

If you were to plot out the counts, you'd see that it makes a kind of curve. Roughly it makes what is often referred to as an invasion curve. An invasion curve starts small and gradually builds, and usually begins to taper off. The tapering is typically due to some form of saturation or symbiotic balance that the invader reaches in the ecosystem.

There are these stages to an invasion curve:

- Prevention

- Eradication

- Containment

- Resource Protection

For prevention, the invader is not yet introduced and so if you don't want the invader to take hold then you put up barriers or take steps to prevent it from emerging into the ecosystem. One could say that the legislation today about self-driving cars is a kind of "preventative" measure, at least with regard to trying to ensure that the self-driving cars are safe for being on the roadways.

Once the invader starts to emerge, the next stage is eradication. Here, the population is still relatively small and it is feasible typically to try and eradicate it before it becomes more pervasive. This could happen with self-driving cars in that if the first set of true self-driving cars begins to falter, such as say hitting other cars or hitting pedestrians, we might see efforts to eradicate the self-driving car.

Now, that being said, it seems like the self-driving car is going to be one of those invaders that is the proverbial letting the genie out of the bottle. It seems unlikely that one could eradicate per se the self-driving car, and instead more likely just prevent it from continuing to spread until the point at which it is able to be proven that it has been changed to be safe (or safer).

In the containment stage, the invader has had a rapid increase in distribution and has become quite abundant in the ecosystem. This could happen with the true self-driving cars. We might have self-driving cars become widely popular, and then, out-of-the-blue, suppose there is some fatal flaw that had not previously been detected. It could put momentary brakes on the continued expansion of self-driving cars. There would likely be public efforts to contain the rise of the self-driving car.

Finally, once an invader has taken deep roots in the ecosystem, it becomes mainly a matter of resource protection. This is somewhat akin to how conventional non-self-driving cars are today. We have all sorts of rules and regulations that provide for our protection and prevent cars from becoming unsafe or at least less safe than they are today.

I realize that most pundits are focused on the adoption curve when it comes to self-driving cars. The notion is that we want to adopt self-driving cars and so let's push it along on the stages of adoption. That's obvious and easy to consider. We've provided a somewhat alternative view that another way to consider self-driving cars is as an invading species.

As such, it is helpful to consider the stages of an invasion curve and consider what we might do if the invader has issues along the way of its insertion into our ecosystem. Certainly, this is a somewhat unconventional way to think of this, but nonetheless helpful when considering the socioeconomic impacts of the true Level 5 self-driving cars. As per the Romans, every new beginning comes from some other beginning's end.

CHAPTER 10

NORMALIZATION OF

DEVIANCE AND

AI SELF-DRIVING CARS

CHAPTER 10

NORMALIZATION OF DEVIANCE
AND AI SELF-DRIVING CARS

The movie "Deepwater Horizon" provides an entertaining and informative glimpse at what transpired in April 2010 that ultimately led to a floating oil drill platform explosion, and generated the worst oil spill ever in the United States. I suppose that I should have said "spoiler alert" and not told you what the outcome of the movie is, but I am guessing that you likely already are aware that the actual oil drilling platform was called Deepwater Horizon and that the movie of the same named depicted the historical events involving the crisis that occurred there.

If you don't know anything about Deepwater Horizon, you might perhaps assume that the explosion and fire onboard the platform was likely due to slip shod work that failed to abide by safety practices and that the crew there had become complacent and careless in their efforts. Would you then be surprised to know that the platform had one of the highest safety records and had gone a nearly unprecedented seven years without any significant accidents? Ironically, the platform crew had just received a special recognition award for their incredible safety accomplishment, receiving it just prior to the deadly explosion that killed nearly a dozen crew members and started a disastrous oil spill that ensued for months.

The crew consisted of seasoned experts. They were known for their safety record. How could they have been so unawares that a major incident was soon to occur. Also, keep in mind that they had practiced and were presumably prepared for all sorts of calamities that could happen on the platform. They routinely practiced various kinds of breakages, accidents, and other snafus that could lead to the platform being disrupted or potentially have a severe problem. They had equipment that provided all sorts of indicators about the status of the platform. They had automatic alerts throughout the systems there, helping to ensure that any kind of anomaly would be detected right away, and the humans running the platform would be warned that something was amiss, so they could take action before a small problem erupted into a big one.

One answer to this confounding paradox is that it might have been due to normalization of deviance.

What's normalization of deviance, you likely are asking? It is a phenomenon of human behavior that we sometimes will allow for small deviations beyond the norm that we shrug off, often due to over confidence, and those small variants begin to add-up until it becomes an overwhelming deviation. You might think of this as a snowball effect, wherein one small aspect leads to another and another, until ultimately, we have a gigantic snowball that plows us under.

Notice that I mentioned that this can occur due to over confidence. Another alternative is that someone might not be astute enough to even realize that the small deviations are occurring. If you have a novice doing a task, they might not realize when something is outside the norm, precisely because they don't yet even know what the norm is. In the case of the Deepwater Horizon, I had mentioned earlier here that the crew was seasoned and experts. They weren't novices. So, unlike novices that we could potentially readily understand why they don't recognize small deviations, in the case of experts it is usually due to their over confidence in their own abilities. They are too smart for their own good, one might say.

You might be tempted to think that maybe these experts were actually so-called amoral calculators. That's a phrase used to describe someone that is not taking into account the morality of their decisions and that opts to purposely undermine or avoid safety precautions.

The famous case of the space shuttle Challenger was at first thought to be an example of tossing safety to the wind by amoral calculating personnel.

Challenger was the shuttle that blew-up shortly after launch, due to rubber seals that had become hardened and brittle during cold weather on the launch day and ended-up leading to a leak that burned a hole into the fuel tank, and the rest is sad history. Much of the media attention afterward went toward the aspect that on the launch day, in spite of knowing about the dangers of cold weather, the decision by NASA to launch must have been due to evil doers that were willing to sidestep safety for the sake of pleasing the media and others that were waiting for the launch.

Turns out that NASA was aware of the seal issues, over an extended period of time, but step by step had believed over time that it was not much of a big deal and could be readily managed (see a great book by sociologist Diane Vaughan entitled "The Challenger Launch Decision" that covers the NASA incident in fascinating detail). They had incrementally deluded themselves into believing that the rubber seals were simply a fact of life that had to be dealt with. And, they believed that it could be dealt with, since prior launches had gone off without a hitch.

For Deepwater Horizon, some analyses of the incident have concluded that the drilling platform destruction and resultant oil spill were the result of years of stretching the envelope. Over time, these floating platforms have been taken into deeper and deeper waters. The technology and the procedures were modestly adjusted to handle the increasingly severe aspects of pressure and other hazards in those deeper waters. It seemed as though they were successfully adjusting since there the Deepwater Horizon had such an unblemished record. We must be doing something right, they figured. Why else are we able to keep taking on higher risks and yet haven't seen any substantial problems arise.

In the end, this over confidence and snowball effect can lead to a sudden and dramatic disaster. Any organization today that tackles complex systems that have the potential for life and death results should be cognizant of the normalization of deviance phenomenon and be on the look for it. Early detection is imperative to catch on, early enough, and realize explicitly that things that are building toward a really bad result.

What does this have to do with AI self-driving cars?

At the Cybernetic Self-Driving Car Institute, we believe that there are auto makers and tech firms developing AI self-driving cars that are potentially undergoing normalization of deviance, and yet they are currently unaware that they are doing so. It could lead to a disastrous result. We have been trying to bring attention to this real and alarming possibility, and also do something about it.

First, keep in mind that right now, there is an arms race of sorts taking place in the AI self-driving car arena. Each day, there is one auto maker or tech firm or another that announces a claimed new breakthrough toward self-driving cars. We've seen that the self-driving car makers are each scampering to get their self-driving cars onto the roadways. The belief is that public perception of who is leading the way will mean that the auto maker or tech firm will become the chosen self-driving car model upon which everyone else will want to have. It's the usual tech industry first-mover way of thinking. Whomever lands on the moon first will grab all the market share, it is assumed.

Unfortunately, this notion is also promoting very aggressive choices in how the AI systems work on self-driving cars. There is not being allowed sufficient time to make carefully considered choices. It's a matter of developing the software, creating the neural network, or whatever, and doing some amount of apparently sufficient testing, and then put it into the real-world.

Now, we are not suggesting that these are amoral calculators. Instead, we are suggesting that just like the Deepwater Horizon example, these are experts that are doing what they do, and doing so with earnest belief in what they are doing. But, along the way, they are shaving corners here and there. Overall, their AI self-driving cars seem to be working, and this bolsters them to make more corner shaving and keep going. Inch by inch, they are building toward an adverse outcome, but for which they don't even realize is coming. They are deluding themselves into thinking that since things are going well, and therefore have the belief that it will continue in that manner.

To-date, any of the incidents involving AI self-driving cars have been pretty much kept quiet. Yes, in some states there are requirements that the self-driving cars being tested on public roads must report their incidents. But, the reporting is usually at a high-level and without any sufficient detail for the general public to know what the incident truly consisted of. Furthermore, most of the self-driving cars have a human engineer in the self-driving car that is there to takeover controls if something goes amiss. In that sense, it further masks what the incident might have been.

As we get nearer to AI self-driving cars on the public roads and that don't have a human engineer waiting breathlessly to take over the vehicle, we are likely to begin to finally see some of the results of the normalization of deviance. The AI will get itself into a pickle and be unable to readily resolve a situation. This notion that the AI should merely slow down the self-driving car and pull off to the side of the road is not going to be sufficient in all cases. There will be cases wherein the self-driving car is going to get into a bad incident and it will potentially be due to the AI system.

Hopefully, when these first bad incidents happen, it will be a wake-up call. If we can all catch the normalization of deviance before it gets overly far along, it might be a means to ensure that all of the auto makers and tech firms will become more introspective of their systems. We might also see more of a movement towards having third-parties that come in and review or audit the AI systems that are being devised for self-driving cars. If it gets bad enough with a sizable number of serious incidents, we might even see regulators that will put in place regulations to combat this.

Right now, the AI self-driving car is the darling of new automation. It appears to have the promise of zero fatalities (a myth that I've spoken about and written about many times), along with other tremendous societal positive impacts. Suppose though that we are in the midst of creating AI self-driving cars that each has hidden disaster points within them. If this continues without being caught early, we could end-up with thousands upon thousands of self-driving cars on the roads that are waiting to have bad results.

I know that you are thinking that we can always just do an over-the-air fix for anything that arises. In other words, most of the AI self-driving cars are being equipped with an ability to update or revise the software on-board the self-driving car via a network connection. Yes, this is a quite handy way to fix things, but imagine if there are thousands upon thousands of AI self-driving cars that need to have these over-the-air fixes. Will the self-driving cars be considered unusable until an adequate fix is available, or will all of those owners be unable to use their vaunted self-driving car until the fix is perfected? How long will it take to derive such a fix? And, if a self-driving car is unable to connect to a network, will it even know that it needs to do an update and thus be cruising around with an adverse known ticking software bomb within it?

Fortunately, the odds of a large-scale disaster similar to a shuttle launch or a drilling platform eruption is relatively low for self-driving cars, primarily because the self-driving cars are of a distributed nature and not one large monolith. In that sense, we are distributing out the risk. When I say this, I don't want though experts and non-experts alike to think that they shouldn't therefore be concerned about normalization of deviance. It's still a true and valid concern for the developers and companies that are making AI self-driving cars.

Early successes with AI self-driving cars will continue to build-up support for pushing forward on this exciting technology. If we have some fatalities and they are due to poorly written code in the AI of the self-driving car, I would bet that the public perception of self-driving cars will rapidly erode. Once the public perception erodes, you can bet for sure that the elected government officials are also going to take a dim view of self-driving cars. It will dampen progress and maybe even derail where things are headed. Let's not let that scenario play out.

Instead, let's make sure that the AI self-driving car makers are watching out for the normalization of deviance. As they say, mistakes, mishaps, and disasters are often socially generated and can be traced to social structures and systems that failed to detect and avert them. Time for AI self-driving car developer and firms to make sure they are attune, especially before someone gets hurt and the brakes are applied to our industry.

CHAPTER 11

GROUPTHINK DILEMMA FOR AI SELF-DRIVING CARS

CHAPTER 11

GROUPTHINK DILEMMA FOR
AI SELF-DRIVING CARS

When I was initially out of college with my bachelor's degree in computer science and electrical engineering, I took a job at a small electronics company that made customized electronic systems using real-time microprocessors for all sorts of interesting and unusual uses. As a new buck into the real-world, I figured it was best for me to do my professional best and allow the wiser and wisdom-laden engineers in their olden thirties to provide guidance as to what we should do in our efforts.

I have numerous important lessons of work and life that occurred over the few years that I was there. We put together new systems that nobody else was doing at the time. We stretched the envelope by mixing together disparate technologies and wrote code that ranged from overarching system control to stuff that had to poke deep down into the operating system to make things work. One minute we were writing using a high-level programming language, and the next we are delving into machine language and assembly language. Our code had to work right, since many of these systems involved interaction with humans and robotic arms or automated gates that could harm a human, plus it all had to meet various real-time timing requirements, so it had to be fast and responsive, besides being safe.

One day, we gathered together the developers and the engineers, and discussed a new project for a client that wanted to use a combination of sonar devices, laser detection devices, and a myriad of other sensors. The head of our engineering group was a strong willed take-no-prisoners kind of manager, and he was known for telling others to do what he said, and no backtalk needed and nor entertained. He acted like he was the all-knowing guru. Admittedly, he'd been there for several years and had shepherded into production some of the most advanced and complex systems that the company had ever made. Let's just say that his reputation preceded him and his mightier than thou attitude had become legendary there.

So, we were all assembled into a cramped conference room, and he laid out the requirements for this new system. I noticed something that I found somewhat curious, indeed maybe disturbing. The layout indicated that the devices would default to being classified as being in a working state. Only if a device reported that it was in a failing state or a mode of error, would we know that the device wasn't working right. In my college engineering and design classes, we had always been exhorted to assume that something doesn't work by default and that until it proves that it is working would we rely upon it. Thus, the approach that the heralded guru was advocating seem to be counter to what I had learned, and seemingly a risky approach to a real-time system design.

Should I speak up? According to the guru, this meeting was not a two-way street, it was a one-way street. He was telling us what it was. We were to then dutifully shuffle away and get to work. I looked around at my fellow workers and wondered if they saw the same potential hole that I thought was obvious. I subtly pointed at the requirement that was the questionable one, and mouthed words to my fellow "prisoners" that maybe it wasn't the wisest way to do things. They looked at me with one those "not now" kind of expressions and convinced me without any verbal utterances that I ought to keep my mouth shut (and maybe my eyes too).

To make matters worse, the strongman head engineer decided that he would go around the room and have each person attending signify whether they understood and seemingly agreed with what was to be done. One by one, he pointed at each attendee. One by one, they each said yes. It was getting closer to me and I was completely baffled about what I should say. If I said yes, wasn't I tacitly and maybe even explicitly agreeing to an engineering no-no? If I said no, would I be punished severely and besides a tongue lashing maybe be tossed out the front door and told to never return?

What would you do?

It wasn't an error that you could say outright was an error per se. I justified in my own mind that saying yes was not really agreeing to something erroneous. It could just have been designed a better way. Also, I figured that getting successfully out of the meeting should become my immediate goal. I could always ask the others after the meeting about what we should consider doing. The new buck ought to not make waves at the wrong time, and maybe there would be a right time that I could do so.

I said yes.

After the meeting, I went and saw various individuals that had attended the meeting. Many agreed with me that the design was essentially flawed, but they felt it wasn't something to raise the red flag about. Let it go, they urged me. Just do your job. It will all work out and no one will ever realize that we had proceeded on something that probably could be better engineered. It was like making hamburgers and maybe we let a few get overly burnt or not perfectly shaped, but hey, no one would get food poisoning from it.

We developed the system. The client wanted to do a trial run of it. The client was very excited about the new system and so we sent one of our engineers to go out and make sure it was properly all connected together and working right. After seeing it work, the client then said that they were going to invite various dignitaries to come and see it work. He was proud of what it did and wanted to show it off.

The next morning, sure enough, according to the engineer that was there, a bunch of dignitaries showed up. The client started to run the system. It ran fine. Then, the client said watch how great the sensors are that it will detect when a something gets in the way (such as a human or some other object). He put a pole into the nearby proximity and started the system again. Guess what? The system knocked it to pieces. Everyone was shocked. Why, this thing was dangerous! People were confused. Our head of marketing (being there to tout how great it was), became furious. How could this have happened?

Upon doing a so-called post-mortem (this just means an afterward analysis of went wrong; please note that no one was harmed by the system), we discovered that during the night, a janitor had come into where the system was installed. The janitor knew that a big showcase was taking place the next day. He opted to make sure he really cleaned well in the area of the system. At one point, he couldn't sweep in one area, and so he disconnected some of the cables, and then forgot to reconnect them.

As you can imagine, we realized that because the system was engineered to assume that the devices were working and connected, the rest of the system did not realize that the janitor had disconnected the devices. If we had designed it to assume that the sensors weren't working (by default), it would have been unable to verify that they were in a working state, and thus the system would have produced an audible alert that the system was not ready for use (and wouldn't have allowed it to start).

We got bit by the engineering aspect of months earlier that had been assumed would never arise as an issue.

Why do I tell this story?

Because it brings up a very important aspect of developing new systems, namely the dangers of groupthink.

You've likely heard about groupthink. It's the circumstance when a group of people fall into a mental trap of all thinking one way. There have been some famous cases of the dangers of groupthink, and perhaps one of the most studied and cited examples is the Cuban Missile Crisis and the Bay of Pigs incident. Studies indicate that the Bay of Pigs fiasco partially can be blamed on the President holding a high-level meeting in which no one was willing to say that what they were going to do was perhaps mistaken.

Why do people that are in a group fall into the groupthink trap? In my case, as I mentioned earlier, I was a junior engineer and software developer and felt that I was supposed to abide by what the seasoned head of engineering told us to do. I caved to peer pressure. I caved to the worry that I would get fired. I caved to the belief that my own expertise was insufficient to override what overwhelmingly everyone else said was ok. I caved to the aspect that the manager didn't want any input. Etc.

This became an important lesson for me, and I subsequently become quite aware of the dangers of groupthink, and found ways to combat it throughout the rest of my career. Indeed, part of the reason that I went back to school and got my MBA, and later my PhD, partially was due to the realization that as a technologically proficient software engineer that I ought to also know and understand how to work in organizations and how to perform in teams and how to lead and manage teams.

What does this have to do with AI self-driving cars?

At the Cybernetic Self-Driving Car Institute, we are making sure that our efforts don't fall into the groupthink trap, and we also are advising auto makers and tech firms that are making AI self-driving cars to be aware of and ensure they don't let groupthink take them down the wrong paths.

There are eight aspects that are often underlying the groupthink phenomena. Well, some researchers say there are more than eight, some say there are less than eight, but anyway I figure let's go over the eight commonly cited ones here to make sure you know what to look for.

1. Invincibility Illusion

You might find yourself in a room of other AI specialists as you are working on the AI self-driving car software and they'll say something like "this neural network works because we've used it before and it always works." It could be that these are seasoned researchers with hefty PhD's and other amazing credentials and that have been using neural networks for years, and they have brought to the auto maker or tech firm their favorite time-tested neural network.

They are so confident that they seem invincible. That's when I make sure to start asking questions. I know you'll need to be careful, and you'll face likely the same kinds of pressures that I did in the past. But, keep in mind that you are in the midst of developing a system that involves life and death consequences. Don't fall for the illusion of invincibility.

2. Must Prove the Contrary

You are in a meeting and the group says that the use of LIDAR (a type of light related radar device) won't provide any added value. The tacit expectation is that everyone agrees, and if you don't agree then you have to provide fifty good reasons why they are "wrong" in their approach. Notice that they didn't have to provide fifty reasons why they are "right" – it's you that needs to disprove them.

The burden to disprove can be daunting. If you feel strongly about whatever the matter is, you'll need to do your homework and come up with a strong case for your side of things.

3. Collective Rationalization

The AI self-driving car team meets and says that even if the camera goes wacky it doesn't matter since the sonar will compensate for it. The group rationalizes that the back-up element of having the sonar is sufficient. No one tries to think it through.

You could gently point out that the camera and the sonar are two quite different kinds of sensors and are capturing different kinds of information. It's an apple and oranges comparison. Also, suppose the sonar also goes wacky – what then?

4. Stereotyping Out-Groups

Suppose the top management of the auto maker doesn't really know much about AI self-driving cars. The developers know that top management is out-of-touch and almost acts like a Dilbert cartoon.

During a meeting among just the developers, someone announces that top management wants the team to add some new safety features into the software to make sure that the system won't mistakenly tell the car to run over pedestrians. The team discards the proclamation because it came from top management. Anything that comes from top management they believe has no merit.

Only in this case, maybe what they are asking does have merit. Even if top management doesn't know why this is needed, you ought to set aside the "source" question and instead examine the idea on its own merits.

5. Self-censorship

Suppose the AI of the self-driving car should cause the car to come to a halt if the system is not getting valid data coming from the vehicle sensors such as the speed of the car and the status of the engine. But, during the group meeting to discuss this aspect, there is an indication that only if the vehicle sensor complains will it be needed to start toward halting the car (this is somewhat akin to my example earlier about the engineering design of sensors).

The group doesn't want to entertain counter-arguments. They are maybe tired and just want to get on with things. You decide to self-censor yourself. You hold back your thoughts. The question will be, can you live with this? Are you willing to potentially be a contributor to something that could one day harm others?

6. Unanimity Delusion

Let's revisit the same case as described under self-censorship. Suppose that no one is asked to offer any second opinion. The meeting might have an implied condition that if no one objects, then everyone agrees.

You might find that if you are willing to break the ice and offer a second opinion, what can happen is that suddenly a torrent of others will jump onto your bandwagon. There's a famous play that was made into an equally famous movie, called Twelve Angry Men, which you ought to watch as an example of how one person speaking up can make a tremendous difference.

7. Dissenters as Perceived Whiners

In some meetings, anyone that speaks in some dissenting fashion will get crushed. They either get crushed by someone that is advocating the other side, or they could get crushed simply because other attendees don't want to debate the topic. Also, sometimes a dissenter is seen as a naysayer that won't be happy with anything. They are just complainers.

For this, you'll need to position yourself not as a complainer or whiner. Instead, try to focus on the facts of the situation. What are the factual reasons that LIDAR can add substantive value to the AI self-driving car that your firm is making? It becomes more bona fide when others realize that it's a systematic discussion rather than just a complaint session.

8. Mindguards

This last one is quite interesting. Sometimes, a meeting will take place and yet a key expert is left out of the meeting. Not by accident, but by design. Whomever has setup the meeting has explicitly decided they don't want the person to attend. It could be because they believe the person is too argumentative, or maybe they just don't like the person.

The problem with this kind of mindguarding is that it means that the meeting will potentially be making decisions that are ill-informed. You don't have in the meeting the needed expertise to make a sound decision.

Here, you can sometimes try to get the group to agree that "let's check with George or Samantha" about whatever has been tentatively decided, allowing for them later access to the expert to help confirm or disconfirm the decision made.

Conclusion

Groupthink could lead an AI self-driving car project into a bad place. The act of meeting together can inadvertently produce adverse results by having decisions made about the hardware and software design that ultimately will undermine the safety or capabilities of the self-driving car. As a developer, you need to be wary of groupthink and try to overcome it. If you are a manager, it is your duty to be aware of groupthink and also try to overcome it. We need self-driving cars that are well designed and well built, and can be safe and usable in the real-world. Don't let groupthink undermine that!

CHAPTER 12

INDUCED DEMAND

DRIVEN BY

AI SELF-DRIVING CARS

CHAPTER 12

INDUCED DEMAND DRIVEN BY AI SELF-DRIVING CARS

For those of you that have lived through multiple generations of computers, you likely know that the amount of memory available on an off-the-shelf computer has steadily increased. It is nearly humorous today to look back at the Radio Shack TRS-80 microcomputer of the mid-1980s and realize that it came with 24KB RAM, which at the time was thought to be a whopping amount of memory. You might recall that when 8 inch floppy drives first appeared in the mid-1970s that people were ecstatic that those gargantuan floppies could hold 800KB. Next along came 5.25 inch floppies that held 1.2MB, and then the 3.5 inch floppies that had 1.44MB. Of course, in modern times we look at a 1TB USB memory stick and seem to think it's not much memory at all.

There is a famous or perhaps infamous quote attributed to Bill Gates in which he allegedly said that "no one will need more than 637K of memory for a personal computer, 640K ought to be enough for anybody." I don't want to be accused of spreading fake news, and so please be aware that Bill Gates has refuted that he said such a thing. There are a number of myth busters that have tried to show that he never said the 640K statement and that it was falsely attributed to him, while others now appear to believe there's an elitist led cover-up underway and he really did say it – a cover-up of the same significance as to maybe we faked the moon landing and perhaps there was a grand conspiracy plot to assassinate JFK.

I'm not going to get mired into that whole debate, and instead my emphasis is that we've seen the amount of computer memory increase greatly over time. And, equally important to my discussion here, we've all seemed to use that memory up. In other words, each time we've gotten more computer memory available, we all seem to find ways to use it. You might at first assume that with the increase in available memory that a lot of it therefore just sits idle and unused. Certainly, there are many that do allow the available memory to be unused, but inch by inch we all seem to eventually use it up

Indeed, there is a popular credo known among most software developers that says this: "Any given program will expand to fill all the available memory." Or, namely that we'll fill computer memory with either programs or data, and every time we get more computer memory, we once again ultimately fill it up. It's axiomatic.

Another way to think of this phenomena is to say that it is induced demand.

Induced demand is an economic theory that postulates there are situations that can possibly spark demand for a resource (it is "induced" to occur). It involves demand and supply. In particular, if the supply of something is increased, then in fact one belief is that more of that supply is consumed, or in other words demand will rise (versus assuming that the existing demand will remain the same, and thus there would then be an "excess" of the now added supply).

One example of the potential impact of induced demand relates to roadways.

Suppose that you have a local freeway that has been getting clogged with traffic. The assumption by most local politicians and even transportation planners is that if you were to expand the local freeway that it would then alleviate the freeway traffic congestion. This seems to make intuitive sense. If a pipe is not able to handle the flow of something (in this case, traffic flow), if you simply enlarge the pipe it seems logical to assume that the traffic will flow more readily. We all know this from our everyday experience of interacting with water flowing in pipes -- get a bigger pipe and the water flows more readily. Obviously!

But, hey, not so fast on that assumption.

New York City is famous for having built at great expense the Triborough Bridge to alleviate traffic congestion that was flummoxing the Queensborough Bridge. At first, it seemed like the new bridge did the trick and the flow on the old bridge improved. Gradually, inexorably, the flow on the old bridge returned to its congested mess, and meanwhile even the new bridge also became a congested mess. In theory, that's not what should have happened, at least in the eyes of the politicians, the transportation planners, and the driving public.

How could this have occurred? Some would argue that it was an example of induced demand, or referred to as "traffic generation" or "induced traffic" or sometimes also described as an example of latent demand. The logic of this argument is that there was demand that wanted to use the bridges but was not doing so, and once the new capacity was added, people perceived that they should go ahead and start driving on the bridges. This then continued until once again the bridge capacities reached their congestion limit, and so any additional latent demand then becomes suppressed and awaits any new supply (more bridges) that might be built.

I can assure you that in Southern California this seems to happen with a frequent and blatantly observable basis. We keep adding additional lanes to our freeways, either by sacrificing an emergency lane or by narrowing existing lanes, and at first we get a moment of congestion relief. In short order, things seem to get gummed up again. This is especially irksome because usually there are promises that once we deal with the agony and delays of the construction to add lanes, it will be worth it since the traffic will improve. Some cynical drivers would say that it wasn't worth the construction woes and there's just no point to these nutty and misguided construction projects, other than falsely appeasing the public and putting construction workers to work.

At times, there is a counter argument that the increase in traffic that ends-up consuming the added supply of roadway is actually traffic being now diverted or switching from some other nearby path. For example, suppose you have a congested freeway and roughly parallel to it there is a highway. Suppose that the traffic on the highway decides to switch over to use the freeway, once they see that the freeway has added capacity. Thus, the reason that the new supply gets consumed is that other traffic has opted to now switch into using the new supply.

If you buy into that argument, you would then say that it wasn't latent demand per se, and instead it was existing demand that has now been diverted over to the new supply. This would also imply that the highway should then exhibit less traffic than it did before, since presumably that traffic is now on the freeway. Well, a number of studies suggest that in most cases the roadway congestion on added roadway capacity cannot be attributed to this switchover traffic. They have not been able to find a commensurate reduction in other traffic that would relate to the newly added capacity of roadway and therefore conclude that the theory of traffic being diverted or switched is not the culprit for the new congestion.

This then brings us back to the theory that it is latent demand. What kind of latent demand would there be, you might ask? Let's suppose that for a freeway that is currently congested that there are drivers that know about the congestion and are not caught off-guard about the congestion. Suppose further that those drivers know that the congestion is primarily from 7 a.m. in the morning until 9:30 a.m. in the morning. This would be the so-called morning rush hour traffic.

Drivers that know about the morning rush hour traffic might decide that they will wait to go to work until after 9:30 a.m. They somehow make a deal with their employer for this. So, they sit at home, waiting until 9:30 a.m., and then they get into their cars and head onto the freeway. This would be considered an example of latent demand with respect to the morning rush hour. Drivers are not driving during the rush hour because they are trying to avoid it. Once the freeway capacity is increased, those drivers might decide that now they are willing to drive during the morning rush hour and so they switch their work starting time to say 8 a.m. and get onto the freeway around 7 a.m.

Furthermore, suppose there are drivers that would like to go and get some breakfast and then return home. But, suppose they know that the freeway is too crowded and so they instead buy cereal on the weekends and eat just some cereal for their breakfasts. But, once the freeway capacity is increased, and if it appears that the congestion has disappeared, they now decide they want a hot breakfast and so go ahead and drive to get it. This is more latent demand. The added supply is prompting drivers to go ahead and use the added supply.

These examples of latent demand are suggestive that the roadway supply is eventually consumed and that this induced travel or traffic generation is the basis for the eventual re-congestion.

Let's return to our economics foundations. The drivers that were in the latent demand camp were perceiving that the "price" of driving during the morning rush hour was too high (they therefore avoided driving during the morning rush hour). Once the supply was increased, the perceived price then dropped. Once the perceived price dropped, the demand to use the supply increased. Eventually, the increase in demand consumed the available supply. Ergo, congestion reappeared.

Other forms of potential latent demand for this situation include:

Drivers that were using alternatives such as bikes or buses, now decide to start using their cars due to the added supply and lessened price.

Drivers decide to make longer driving trips and so use more of the supply than they had driven before.

Drivers decide to make more frequent trips, doing several hops, whereas before they might have only been willing to bear a single longer trip on the roadway that was congested.

And so on.

You might be tempted to conclude that we should never increase roadway capacity because all that will happen is that it will be entirely consumed and we'll be back to a congested state. That's not quite the right kind of thinking here. There are many circumstances whereby increasing the roadway capacity might not lead to furtherance of congestion. All that this is pointing out is that we cannot assume that any added roadway will guarantee a reduction in traffic congestion. We need to be aware of and be contemplating the potential for latent demand, which might or might not happen, and might be small or might be large, depending on the specific situation. Trying to make sweeping generalizations that any added roadway capacity will always lead to more congestion is rather nonsensical and certainly misleading.

What does this have to do with AI self-driving cars?

At the Cybernetic Self-Driving Car Institute, we are running simulations about the future of traffic when there are AI self-driving cars on the roadways. This is important for many technological, social, economic, and political reasons to be given due and serious consideration.

Right now, there are self-driving car pundits that are saying we will have zero traffic congestion once we have AI self-driving cars. They paint a rather rosy picture of how wonderful the roads will be. No more bumper to bumper traffic. No more morning or afternoon rush hour clogs. It will be a beautiful sight of self-driving cars flowing at maximum speeds and it will be a breeze to get from one part of town to the other.

This painted picture is appealing to everyone. Politicians are motivated to support self-driving cars. Transportation planners love it. The public is excited to see this all happen. Let's not wait one minute more. Get those congestion freeing AI self-driving cars on the roads, and like so much Drano will relieve the existing horrors of traffic congestion.

But, hey, not so fast!

Remember the whole discussion herein about latent demand and how it impacts added roadway supply. Let's consider how that might apply.

Part of the reason that some are so excited about self-driving cars is because it will allow those that otherwise cannot readily drive a car to be able to driven around in a car. This might be elderly that aren't able to drive, this might be those that are disabled that aren't able to drive, and so on. You could even say that this includes children – there are many that believe we'll be putting our children into AI self-driving cars and sending them to school via that means, rather than having to go with them as an adult and drive them to school.

We could consider all of those existing non-drivers as latent demand. Once the AI self-driving car is readily available, there will presumably be a ton of latent demand that will come out of the woodwork.

Will our existing roadways be able to handle this?

Might all of these AI self-driving cars radically increase the number of cars on the roadways, and the number of miles driven, and the number of trips taken? It sure seems like it will. Essentially, we are "reducing" the "price" of driving in the sense that those that could not otherwise afford to be driven before (due to the cost of say hiring a chauffeur), will now be able to "afford" the cost to be driven around. This decrease in pricing will increase the demand, which will soak up the supply of roadways.

You might say that ridesharing has already started us down this same path. By having available Uber and Lyft and other ridesharing services, the cost to be driven around has been reduced, at least in terms of the access to ridesharing versus the prior taxi-led approach which had all sorts of frictional costs involved.

AI self-driving cars will presumably boost ridesharing exponentially.

Anyone that owns an AI self-driving car is possibly going to be using their self-driving car as their own personal ridesharing service for others to pay to use. You don't have to be an Uber or Lyft driver. You just somehow advertise that your AI self-driving car is available for ridesharing and voila you can make money off your AI self-driving car.

This is why Uber and Lyft are furiously trying to get into self-driving cars themselves, since they can see the handwriting on the wall that their existing business model of having human drivers is going to eventually go away and they could therefore be another example of a disrupted industry by a new technology (in this case, the AI self-driving car). Will such ridesharing services simply be the conduit to connect those that own AI self-driving cars that want to make available their self-driving car for ridesharing with those that need a lift? Couldn't a Facebook do this instead? That's what scares all of the existing ridesharing services.

Think also about other ways that AI self-driving cars might increase driving.

Some are saying that you could move out of the downtown city area and live in the suburbs, because with an AI self-driving car you can have it pick you up in the morning, you sleep on the way to work, and no need to worry about that morning commute. Our whole pattern of where we live and where we work could change. Distance between us and work, or us and the mall (if malls still exist!), and so on, won't really matter since we have an AI self-driving car that will take us wherever we want to go. You don't need to know how to drive. You don't need to stay awake and be able to drive for ten hours straight. You won't need to find a back-up driver so you can switch during long trips. It's all driving being done by the AI.

You might decide to ditch taking the bus. You might not ride your bike. You might instead decide to go in that cool AI self-driving car instead. The amount of latent demand is potentially enormous. The AI self-driving car might become the most traffic inducing, traffic generator of all time.

We should be careful in assuming that AI self-driving cars will get us to the vaunted zero congestion.

No matter how well the AI self-driving cars drive, and how well coordinated they are, volume is still volume.

There are some that criticize the induced demand theory as somewhat hogwash-like in that the critics claim that when roadways are expanded and become clogged it isn't the traveling that causes this, but instead there is an economic benefit that people must perceive and so the basis for their traveling. If people get into their cars and are driving on these expanded roadways, it is presumably because they see an economic benefit in doing so. Therefore, the increase in cars on the roadways is a good thing in that people are gaining more economic benefit. People are traveling for a purpose and we need to consider the larger picture of how economically there is a collective benefit involved. I won't take the space and time here to detail their argument, but want to at least make you aware of it and you can then postulate it and consider researching more about it, if you like. In short, if indeed AI self-driving cars produces congestion, it in a sense is a reflection that we'll have a lot more people gaining economic benefit by making those driving trips than otherwise if they didn't.

Let me give you a personal example of how this induced demand might impact someone's driving and miles traveled. When my children were in middle school, I used to drive them to school in the morning (this was a delight to do, and I miss it dearly!). Suppose we use the letter M to represent my son, and the letter L to represent my daughter. My son has a friend that we'll label G, and my daughter has a friend we'll label S. We had a custom of getting bagels and donuts in the morning, and I'll label the donut shop as D.

Here was a daily morning commute:

$$(M+L) + G + S + D$$

This meant that M and L got into our car, I drove us to pick-up my son's friend G, we then drove to pick-up my daughter's friend S, and then we stopped at the D to get some grub. We used my car to do so this, so we have 1 vehicle, or V1. The distance traveled was 3 miles in total.

Let's represent this as:

$$V1: (M+L) + G + S + D = 3 \text{ miles}$$

Now, somedays, my daughter was behind schedule (time was a

key factor in these morning trips!), and it was prudent to go ahead and do this:

V1: M + G + L + S + D = 5 miles

This shows that M got into the car with me, we went and picked up his friend G, we came back to the home to get L, we then went to get S, and then to D. The total miles is now 5 miles, because of the trip to get G and come back to our house. It was worth the extra distance because we were trying to beat the clock.

Some mornings, I would get up really early, and do this:

V1: D + (M + L) + G + S = 7 miles

I would go get the D grub, then drive back home, and proceed with the rest of the sequence. The number of miles of the morning trip has now risen to 7 miles. It made sense because I then had the D in-hand and this saved us time once the rest of the sequence occurred.

Some mornings, we were running late, and we'd ask the parents of G and of S to drop-off their kids at our house:

V3: [G] + [S] + (M+L) + D = 10 miles

Notice now that we had three cars involved, including the cars of the parents for G and S. This now makes what otherwise would have been a 3 mile trip into a now 10 mile trip.

How does this relate to AI self-driving cars?

The odds are that this 10 mile trip would be the likely candidate once we have AI self-driving cars. We would either send our AI self-driving car to go get G and S and bring them to our house, or maybe the parents would send their kids to our house via their AI self-driving cars.

The point is that with AI self-driving cars it will be much easier to go ahead and have a driving trip undertaken. It seems very likely that the number of trips, the length of trips, and the number of miles traveled are going to go up, probably a lot.

What we don't yet know is what will be the cost of the AI self-driving cars? Right now, everyone seems to be assuming, either implicitly or explicitly, that the cost of the AI self-driving car is about the same as driving any conventional car. Suppose though that the cost of a self-driving car is a lot higher than conventional cars? This could increase the "price" of making use of self-driving cars and therefore not lead us down the path of the price decrease (which led us to the demand increase and the supply consumption). When you consider a conventional car, you acknowledge that having a human driver means there's an additional price or cost associated with the use of the car. Is it the case that the AI self-driving car "driver" will be less than that cost, the same as, or more than that cost?

We've been running various simulations, taking a look at mixtures of the price aspects, along with also considering the mix of human driven cars versus AI self-driving cars. I say this because it is unrealistic to assume that suddenly one day we will have instantaneously all self-driving cars on the road. We won't. We instead will have a mix of both human driven cars and AI driven cars.

Eventually, presumably, the number of AI driven cars will gradually overtake the number of human driven cars, and maybe someday it will only be AI driven cars (there's a lot of controversy on that point!). Anyway, all of us need to put some sober, serious thought toward the future of our car travel and consider how this will impact our habits, how we live, where we live, the roadways, and the rest. It's an issue, a large problem to be dealt with, and the platitudes of "zero congestion" need to be carefully scrutinized, and in fact maybe we should substitute instead the more thought provoking phrase of "induced demand."

CHAPTER 13

COMPRESSIVE SENSING
FOR
AI SELF-DRIVING CARS

CHAPTER 13

COMPRESSIVE SENSING

FOR AI SELF-DRIVING CARS

Years ago, I did some computer consulting work for a chemical company. It's quite a curious story and one that went into the record books as a consulting engagement. The way it began was certainly an eye opener.

An executive at a company that I had been doing consulting for had been golfing with an executive from a chemical company and they got to discussing computers during their round of golf. The chemical company executive expressed that he was looking for a good consultant that would keep things confidential and be very discrete. The exec that I knew told him that I fit that mold. I received the next day an out-of-the-blue call from the assistant to the chemical executive and was asked if I would be interested in coming out to their company for a potential consulting gig.

I jumped at the chance as it was rare to have a prospect call me, versus my having to try and beat the bushes to find new clients. I dutifully showed-up at the appointed date and time, wearing my best suit and tie. The lobby assistant escorted me back into the office area and as we walked through the halls of the building, I noticed a set of double doors that had a rather prominent sign that said "No Admittance Unless Authorized." I assumed that there must be some kind of special chemicals or maybe company secrets that were locked behind those doors.

Upon entering into the office of the executive, he warmly greeted me. We sat and had some initial small talk. I could see that he wanted to tell me something but was hesitating to do so. I decided to mention that my work is always of a confidential nature and that I don't talk about my clients (note: I realize that my telling the story now might seem untoward, but it was many years ago that this client activity occurred and I am also purposely leaving out any specific details).

He then confided in me an incredible tale. Here's what the scoop was. They were a tiny division of a very large chemical company. Headquarters had decided to try and have this division do some analyses of certain chemicals that the company was using. The division would place the chemicals into vials, and run tests on the liquid in the vials. From these tests, they would end-up with ten numbers for each vial. They were to do some statistical analysis on the numbers and provide a report to headquarters about their findings.

The division was excited to receive this new work from HQ. They had hired a software developer to create an application for them that would allow by-hand entry of the vial numbers and would calculate the needed statistics, along with producing a report that could be sent back to headquarters. The developer was one of those one-man-band kind of programmers and had whipped out the code quickly and cheaply. So far, the tale seems rather benign.

Here's the kicker. Turns out that the software wasn't working correctly. First of all, upon entering the ten numbers for each vial, somehow the program was messing up and on the reports it showed different numbers than were entered. They also discovered that the statistics calculations were incorrect. Even the manner that the ten numbers needed to be entered was goofy and it allowed easily for the data entry people to enter the wrong values. There was no internal error checking in the code. The ten numbers were always to be in the range of 1 to 20, but a user could enter any number, such as say 100 or -100, and the code would allow it. The data entry people were pretty sloppy and were also time pressured to enter the numbers, leading to a ton of bad data getting into the otherwise bad program overall.

You've probably heard about a famous computer industry expression: Garbage In, Garbage Out (GIGO). It means that if you let someone enter lousy data, you are likely going to see lousy data coming out of the system. There are many programs and programmers that don't seem to care about GIGO and their attitude is often "if the user is stupid enough to enter bad data, they get what they deserve!" That being said, in contrast there are programmers that do care about GIGO, but they are sometimes told not to worry about it, or not given enough time and allowed effort to write code to stop or curtail GIGO.

In contemporary times, the mantra has become GDGI, which stands for Garbage Doesn't Get In. This means that the developers of a program should design, build, and test it so that it won't allow bad data to get into the program. The sooner that you can catch bad data at the entry point, the better off you are. The further that bad data makes its way through a program, the harder it is to detect, the harder it is to stop, and the harder it is to correct (as a rule of thumb).

Let's get back to the story. The division executive had discovered that the program was cruddy, and that the data was bad, doing so before they had sent any of the reports to headquarters. The programmer though was nowhere to be found. He was not responding to their requests that he come and rewrite the application. After trying to reach him over and over, they found a different programmer and asked to have the code rewritten. This programmer said that the code was inscrutable and there wasn't going to be any viable means of fixing it.

Meanwhile, the division was under the gun to provide the reports. They did what "anyone" might do -- they decided to calculate the statistics by hand. Yes, they abandoned using the application at all. They instead bought a bunch of calculators and hired temporary labor to start crunching numbers. They then had this written up in essentially Word documents and sent those over to headquarters. In doing so, they implied that they had a program that was doing the calculations and keeping track of the data. It was hoped that headquarters wouldn't figure out the mess that the division had really gotten itself into, and buy them time to figure out what to do.

The reason they had the double doors with the big sign about no admittance unless authorized was due to the fact that each day they had hordes of temps that were coming into the room there to do all of these by-hand calculations. They were trying to keep it a secret even within the division itself. The executive told me that he was not able to sleep at nights because he figured that the ruse would eventually be uncovered by others. He had gotten himself into quite a mess.

You can probably now see why he was looking for a computer consultant that had discretion.

The main reason I tell the story here is that I wanted to discuss GIGO and GDGI. Before I do so, I'll go ahead and provide you with the happy ending to the story. I was able to rewrite the application, we got it going, and eventually the data was being stored online, the calculations were being done correctly, and we had lots of error checking built into the code. Headquarters remained pleased, and indeed even dramatically increased the volume of chemical tests coming to the division. Had we not gotten the software fixed up, the division would have had to hire most of the population of the United States just to do the by-hand statistical calculations.

Anyway, one lesson here is that sometimes you want to allow data to flow into an application, freely, and deal with it once its already inside. In other cases, you want to stop the data before it gets into the application per se, and decide what to do with it before it gets further along in the process.

Allow me to switch topics for the moment and discuss compressive sensing.

Compressive sensing is a technique and approach to collecting data from sensors. If you take a look at all of the sensors on an AI self-driving car, which might have a dozen cameras, a dozen sonars, a LIDAR, and so on, you begin to realize that those sensors are going to generate a ton of data. The deluge of data coming into the AI self-driving car system is going to require hefty computational processing and a huge amount of storage. The more you need computational processing then the more processors you need in the AI self-driving car, and likewise the more computer storage that you'll need. This adds cost to the AI self-driving car, along with adding weight, along with adding complexity, along with adding the chances for breakdowns and other problems.

In today's world, we assume that all of the data coming from those sensors is precious and required. Suppose that a camera has taken a picture and it consists of one million pixels of data. All one million of those pixels are collected by the sensor and pushed forward into the system for use and analysis. The computational processing needs to examine one million pixels. The internal memory needs to store the one million pixels.

We often deal with torrents of data by using various compression techniques and programs. Typically, the compression algorithm does encoding to undertake the compression, and then does decoding when the compressed data needs to be brought back into its uncompressed state. A completely lossless compression is one that returns you back the same thing exactly that you started with. A lousy compression is one that will not guarantee that you can get back your original, since during the compression it might do things that will prevent you from reconstructing the original.

The compression involves the usual trade-off of time and quality. A faster compression algorithm tends to reduce the quality or losslessness of the result. Also, there are trade-offs about whether you want the most time to be consumed when doing the encoding, or at the decoding. If you have data coming into you at a really fast pace, you often cannot afford to do much encoding, and so you use a "dumb encoder" that won't take long to run. You tend to pay for this in that when you do the decoding, often considered "smart decoding" it then takes a while to run, but that might be OK because you were pressed for time when the data first arrived and in contrast maybe have a lot more time to deal with the decoding.

You can think of the compressive sensing as a means of using a dumb encoder and allowing then for a smart decoder. Part of the reason that the encoder in compressive sensing can go quickly is because it is willing to discard data. In fact, compressive sensing says that you don't even need to collect a lot of that data at all. They view that the sensor designers are not thinking straight and are assuming that every bit of data is precious. This is not always the case.

Suppose that instead of collecting one million pixels for a picture, we instead either told the sensor to only collect 200,000 pixels (the pixels to be chosen at random), or that we let the camera provide the one million pixels but we then selected only 200,000 at random from the array provided. If the image itself has certain handy properties, especially sparsity and also incoherence, we have really good chance of being able to reconstruct what the million must have been, even if we had tossed away the other 800,000 pixels.

The compressive sensing works best when the original data exhibits sparsity, meaning that it has essentially simple elements that are readily composed of the same kinds of nearby pixel values. If the data is noisy and spread all around in a wild manner (like say a lot of static on a TV screen that is widely dispersed), it makes compressive sensing not so handy. Randomness of the original data is bad in this case. We want there to be discernable patterns.

Imagine a painting that has a girl wearing a red dress and there is a blue sky behind her. If we were to outline the girl, we'd see that there are lots of red pixels within the bounds of that outline. When looking outside the outline, we'd see there are lots of blue pixels. If we were to randomly sample the pixels, we would mainly end-up with red pixels and blue pixels. Wherever we saw red pixels in our sample, the odds are that there are more red pixels nearby. Wherever we saw blue pixels, the odds are that there are more blue pixels nearby. In that sense, even if we only had say 20% of the original data, we could pretty much predict where the missing 80% is going to be red pixels or the blue pixels. Kind of a paint-by-numbers notion.

So, via compressive sensing, we have a good chance of starting with just a tiny sample of data and being able to reconstruct what the entire original set must have been. This technique involves a combination of mathematics, computer science, information theory, signal processing, etc. It works on the basis that most of the data being collected is redundant and we don't really need it all. It would seem wasteful to go to the trouble to collect something that is redundant and instead just collect a fraction of it. As they say in compressive sensing, there are way too many measurements often being taken and what we should be doing is simplifying the data acquisition and then following it up with some robust numerical optimization.

With compressive sensing, you take random measurements, rather than measuring everything. You then reconstruct using typically some kind of linear programming or other non-linear minimization function. In a sense, you are trying to simultaneously do signal acquisition and compression. The sensing is considered ultra-efficient and non-adaptive, and recovery or reconstruction is by tractable optimization. If you are used to the classical Nyquist/Shannon sampling approach, you'll find the use of compressive sensing quite interesting and impressive. Its initial roots were in trying to aid medical MRI's and speed-up the processing, reducing therefore the difficulty factor for the human patient in terms of having to sit still for a lengthy time to do an MRI.

What does this have to do with AI self-driving cars?

At the Cybernetic Self-Driving Car Institute, we are using compressive sensing to deal with the deluge of data coming from the numerous sensors on AI self-driving cars.

Right now, most of the auto makers and tech companies developing AI self-driving cars are handling the torrent of data in the usual old fashioned manner. They don't really care about how much processing is needed and nor how much storage is needed, since they are developing experimental cars and they can put whatever souped-up processors and RAM that they want. The skies the limit. No barrier to costs.

Eventually, ultimately, we all will want AI self-driving cars to become available for the masses, and so the cost of the AI self-driving car must come down. One way to get the cost down will be to be more mindful of how fast the processors are and how many you need, and likewise how much memory you need. Currently, most are just trying to get the stuff to work. We're looking ahead to how this stuff can be optimized and minimized, allowing the costs and complexity to be reduced.

Some of the sensor makers are also beginning to see the value of compressive sensing. But, it is a tough choice for them. They don't want to provide a camera that only gives you 200,000 pixels per picture when someone else's camera is giving 1,000,000. It would seem to make their camera inferior. Also, admittedly, the nature of the images being captured can dramatically impact whether the compressive sensing is viable and applicable.

Even though I have been mentioning images and a camera, keep in mind that compressive sensing can apply to any of the sensors on the AI self-driving car. The data could be radar, it could be LIDAR, it could be sonar, it really doesn't matter what kind of data is coming in. It's more about the characteristics of the data as to whether it is amenable to using compressive sensing.

Another reason why compressive sensing can be important to AI self-driving cars is that the speed at which the torrent of data needs to be analyzed can be aided by using compressive sensing. If the AI of the self-driving car is not informed quickly enough by the sensors and sensor fusion about the state of the car, the AI might not be able to make needed decisions on a timely basis. Suppose that an image of a dog in front of the self-driving car has been received by the camera on the self-driving car, but it takes a minute for the image to be analyzed, and meanwhile the AI is allowing the self-driving car to speed forward. By the time that the sensor fusion has occurred, it might be too late for the AI self-driving car to prevent the car from hitting the dog.

Via compressive sensing, if we are able to either not care about receiving all the data or at least we are willing to discard a big chunk of it, the speed at which the sensors report the data and the sensor fusion can happen is possible to be sped up. This will not always be the case and you need to realize that this is not some kind of magical silver bullet.

I had mentioned earlier that the adage of Garbage In, Garbage Out has been around for a while. In one sense, the redundant data that comes to a sensor can be considered as "garbage" in that we don't need it.

I'm not saying that it is bad data (which is what the word "Garbage" in the GIGO context implies). I am merely saying that it is something we can toss away without necessarily fears of doing so. That's why the Garbage Doesn't Get In (GDGI) is more applicable here. The use of compressive sensing says that there's not a need to bring in the data that we otherwise consider redundant and can be tossed out. I urge you to take a look at compressive sensing as it is still a somewhat "new" movement and continues to have room to grow. We firmly believe that it can be very valuable for the advent of widespread and affordable AI self-driving cars. That's a goal we can all get behind!

CHAPTER 14

NEURAL LAYER EXPLANATIONS FOR AI SELF-DRIVING CARS

CHAPTER 14

NEURAL LAYER EXPLANATIONS FOR AI SELF-DRIVING CARS

When my son and daughter were young, I thought it would be handy for them to learn something about how cars work. My father had taught me the basics and had me do things like change the oil on our family cars and sometimes do more complex activities such as changing the spark plugs. I admit freely that I was never trained to be a car mechanic and so please don't ask me to overhaul your car's engine. Let's just say that I understood and was able to explain the essentials of how a car engine worked and could also reasonably carry on discourse about the fundamentals of cars. By the way, my dad said it would impress girls, and so that was quite a motivator.

Anyway, I figured that my own children ought to also know something about how cars work. Kind of like passing along knowledge from one generation to the next. Of course, its harder these days to do much on a car engine because of the automation now integrated into the engine and also how well protected the engine parts are from everyday tinkering consumers. So, I resolved that my intent was just to familiarize them with cars and especially the foundation of how conventional engines work.

I opened the hood of the car (which is more than most kids seem to see these days!), and pointed out the essentials of what the engine consisted of. I realized that it was not making a tremendous impression upon them. This is the case partially because the engine wasn't running at that moment and so they couldn't see any action happening, and also because there are so many other shielding type of elements that you really cannot see the inner areas of the engine. Even when starting the car so that the engine was running, there still wasn't a lot that the naked eye could directly see. I decided that I somehow needed to take them inside the engine.

Well, besides potentially using a super shrinking ray that would make us really tiny (think of "Honey, I Shrunk the Kids"), I remembered that when I was young that I had gotten one of those model engine kits. It allows you to put together plastic parts that represent various elements of a car engine. Once you've put it together, you hook it to a small battery and watch as the engine does its thing. The plastic parts are mainly transparent and so you can see a little piston going up and down, you can see the timing belt linking the crankshaft and the camshaft, and so on. It was a blast when I was a kid and I thought it would a handy tool for teaching my kids about car engines.

Fortunately, I found that they still make those plastic engine model kits, bought one, and with the help of my children we put it together as a family project (better than doing jigsaw puzzles, so they said). When we finally got it to work, which wasn't as easy as I had anticipated, we watched in amazement as the little engine ran. Exciting! It allowed me to further explain how engines work, and made it seem more real by looking at the components of the model kit that we had put together (I realize it might seem odd that a model helped to make something seem more real, but it does make sense).

Now, the kids came up with an interesting idea that I had not considered. They decided to disconnect some elements to see what impact it had on the engine. This was a clever way of ensuring that they understood the nature and purpose of each of the elements. By disconnecting one item, they could see what would happen and it reinforced or at times changed their thinking about how things worked in the engine. They reached a point where they eventually could predict what would occur if you disconnected any piece of the engine. I realized it was a clever way to get a sense of whether they not only understood the individual components, but also that they understood the whole picture of how everything worked together. Double exciting!

Let's switch topics for the moment and discuss machine learning for AI self-driving cars. Don't worry, we'll revisit my story about the plastic model car engine. You'll see.

With many of the budding AI self-driving cars, there is the use of machine learning as a key aspect of creating the ability for AI to drive a car. Usually making use of artificial neural networks, the developers of the AI self-driving cars get a bunch of data and use machine learning to have the system become able to drive a car. Normally, the neural network consists of layers of nodes that we consider suggestive of neurons, though much more simplistic, and the neural network finds patterns in the collected data. The data might be for example images from cameras on a self-driving car and the neural network is trained to discern pedestrians, street signs, dogs, fire hydrants, and so on.

Sometimes the neural network will consist of thousands and upon thousands of neurons. The number of layers can be small, such as a few dozen, or could be hundreds for a millions sized neurons type of neural network. In a general way, this is somewhat akin to how the human brain seems to operate, though the human brain is many orders of magnitude larger and more complex. We still don't really know how the human brain is able to do everything from driving a car to composing music, and in the case of artificial neural networks we are simplistically borrowing from what we kind of think the human brain is partially doing.

The thing that's somewhat disconcerting is that when putting together a sizable artificial neural network, it does some incredible mathematical patterning about the data, but by-and-large if we all looked closely at the neurons, their weights, the synapses or connections, and the layers, we would not have any idea of why it is able to detect the patterns that it has found. In a sense, the typical artificial neural network of a sizable nature becomes a kind of mathematical black box. Sure, you can look at a particular neuron and see that it has such-and-such numeric connections and weights, but you could not directly say that it is there for a specific purpose such as it identifies say the body of a dog in an image captured by the self-driving car camera.

Some say that we don't need to know why the neural network is able to work and that we should just be happy that the advances in developing neural networks has gotten us a lot further along in being able to develop AI self-driving cars. If it works, leave it be. What ain't broken, no need to fix. That might seem like an alluring notion, but it really is not very satisfying. Besides our innate human curiosity, it could also be vital to know why the various aspects of the neural network work the way they do. Suppose that the neural network falsely identifies a dog when the image really consists of a fire hydrant? You won't be able to say why the neural network goofed-up. Those that say no explanation is needed would argue that you should just retrain the neural network, and they continue to insist that your best bet is to treat the neural network as a black box.

At the Cybernetic Self-Driving Car Institute, we don't buy into the black box approach and instead say that we all should be able to interrogate an artificial neural network and be able to explain why it does what it does.

Indeed, as an expert witness in court cases involving computer related disputes, I am already predicting that once we have AI self-driving cars getting into accidents, which mark my words is going to happen, there will be a big backlash against AI self-driving cars, and people are going to want to know why things went awry. There will be lawsuits, for sure, and there will be experts called upon to explain what the system was doing and why it got involved in a car accident. If the experts just shrug their shoulders and say that the black box neural network did it, and can't explain how or why, it isn't going to be good times for the AI self-driving car future.

As such, we are proponents of recent efforts to try and get toward explanations of how and why a neural network works. Again, I don't mean the mathematical aspects. I mean instead the logical aspects of what aspects of the neural network do what. As an example of what I mean, there's a handy research paper entitled "Evaluating Layers of Representation in Neural Machine Translation on Part-of-Speech and Semantic Tagging Tasks" that was done by MIT Computer Science and AI Lab members that provides an indication of some of the state-of-the-art on devising explanations of neural networks.

Their approach is similar to others that are trying to crack open the inner secrets of sizable neural networks. Generally, one of the more promising approaches consists of taking the sizable neural network and trying to review each layer, one layer at a time. You can either turn-on a means of essentially watching the layer operate, or, cleverly instead you extract the layer and put it into a new neural network. You then pump data into the new neural network and see what this isolated ayer does. Out of this aspect, you are maybe able to figure out the logical purpose of that specific layer. You do this with each layer and maybe end-up having an understanding for each layer of the sizable neural network.

This has kind of worked for neural networks that are setup to do speech recognition or that do language translation of say English to French. It appears that the layers are often doing their translative functions by becoming hierarchically based. One layer for example might be down at the lowest level and be identifying the particular sound and what word it fits to, and the next layer might be a step higher in terms of it looks at words in a sentence, and the next layer further higher that starts to peg the word to a targeted translation word, and so on. Another way to describe this is that the layers are arranged from encoders to decoders, and that the raw input passes through the layers and becomes more semantically enriched in terms of the translation effort as it goes from one layer to the next.

Notice that the key trick involved here consists of isolating a layer and trying to figure out what the isolated layer does. Okay, you'll like this, now let's tie this to my story about my kids and the plastic model car engine. Remember how they opted to disconnect a particular element of the model car engine and see what would happen? This is the same concept being used by today's AI and Machine Language researchers that are trying to explain the nature and function of sizable neural networks. Disconnect a piece and take a close look at that piece.

Now, in the case of my kids, they weren't so much focused on the element that was disconnected as they were on what impact the disconnected element had on the rest of the model car engine.

This brings us to the aspects of the upcoming future efforts that are being worked on right now to try and understand what the black box of artificial neural networks is doing.

The divide and conquer strategy to figure out a neural network is handy. Some say that this though might not lead to discovering what the logical basis for parts of the neural network are about. If you look at just one layer, they say, it might be that you cannot figure out its logical purpose. Maybe that layer isn't really just one cohesive comprehensible thing. The layers as a form of grouping of the neural network might be like taking a car engine and just arbitrarily slicing parts of it, and then try to figure out from those random slices what the car engine is doing. It won't get you anywhere toward a logic-based explanation, they say.

Indeed, some say that it's the classic the-sum-is-greater-than-the-parts. Maybe the neural network on an isolated by-layer basis does not have any logic that we can discern. It might go beyond our human derived sense of logic. The mathematical operation is not necessarily going to become a cleanly discernable logical explanation, and in fact the totality of the neural network is really the key. If you accept this argument, you then are back to the notion that it doesn't make sense to try and get into the parts of the neural network to figure out what it does logically.

Another viewpoint is to try and slice the neural network in some other manner. Maybe you are to find a virtual layer that encompasses multiple actual layers of the neural network. The virtual layer could be able to collect together otherwise disparate and seemingly dispersed parts of the neural network and thus be able to logically explain things.

There are some that believe size is the key. For them, the larger the neural network, the less likely they believe that you will be able to find a logic to the neural network. It has become an unruly overgrown tree, and there's no point at trying to look at particular limbs and find logic, nor does it make sense to collect limbs together in something we might consider layers and hope that it is logically purposed.

Others claim that the larger the neural network, the greater chance of identifying the logical elements. Their view is that the smaller neural network must cram together things that aren't seemingly logically to be combined, while a larger sized neural network does lead to specialization that bears upon logical explanation.

Another viewpoint is that the human designer of the neural network that decided on how many layers to use, well, they obviously had in mind a logic and so in the end all you are going to do is come back to that logic of why the neural network operates as it does.

In whatever manner you consider the matter, those that say we aren't going to find a means to logically explain a sizable neural network are kind of throwing in the towel before we've even tried.

Our viewpoint is that we do need to try a myriad of avenues to get toward logical explanations of neural networks. And, as an aside, we suggest that doing so will ultimately likely help us to explain the true "wetware" neural network of them all, the human brain.

In the meantime, let's all keep trying to crack open the mystery of sizable neural networks, and especially when they are used in AI self-driving cars. Please keep in mind that if the general public knew that there were AI self-driving cars on the roadways that had these AI-based black boxes in them, and for which no one really knew logically why they worked, I would think it would diminish the overall fondness for AI self-driving cars.

I suppose you could say that the Uber driver or Lyft driver is in the same boat, namely that we cannot say for sure how their brains are operating and thus how they able to drive a car for us when we do ridesharing, but I think we as humans accept that aspect about other humans, while for AI self-driving cars we have a different set of expectations, fair or not. We all want to know what the AI knows.

CHAPTER 15

SELF-ADAPTING RESILIENCY FOR AI SELF-DRIVING CARS

CHAPTER 15

SELF-ADAPTING RESILIENCY

FOR

AI SELF-DRIVING CARS

Have you ever seen a brittle star? I'm not talking about stars in the night time sky – I'm referring to the ocean-going type of star. The brittle star is an ophiuroid that crawls along the sea floor. The crawling motion is undertaken by the use of its five arms, each of which can ultimately grow to a size of about two feet. These arms are generally slender in shape and are used in a whipping like manner to bring about locomotion for the creature. You can take a look at YouTube videos of brittle stars crawling around, if you'd like to get a better sense of how it moves (I assure you this would be more interesting than watching another cat video!).

What makes the brittle star particularly intriguing is that if one of its arms gets torn off by a predator, the harmed brittle star is still able to crawl around. The brittle star appears to adjust itself to accommodate that there are only four arms leftover rather than five. This adjustment happens nearly immediately, and the brittle star can continue crawling along without having to do much about the lose of one arm. As far as we know, the brittle star does not have to ponder at length what to do about a lost limb. It seemingly readjusts almost spontaneously.

Researchers believe that the brittle star uses its decentralized control mechanism to self-coordinate the movement of its arms, and that mysteriously the decentralized control is able to readjust when an arm is no longer available. This is resiliency of design in nature. I say that it works mysteriously because there is still much open research going on about how biologically this occurs in the brittle star. In spite of our not knowing how it biologically happens, we can certainly witness that it does. A team of researchers in Japan recently developed a robot that acts like a brittle star and tries to showcase how to adapt to physical damage such as the lose of an arm (led by Professor Akio Ishiguro at Tohoku University's Research Institute of Electrical Communication). This kind of biomimicry is a handy means to extend the capability of robots and we often borrow feature and functions that we see in living organisms to improve what robots and AI can do.

The researchers used a synthetic approach to try and deduce how the decentralized control mechanism works. By creating a prototype brittle star robot, they were able to try and mimic the anatomical and behavioral aspects of a real brittle star. Someday we might be able to delve deeply into the neurons and muscles of real brittle stars and gauge how they really work, but in the meantime the robotic brittle star uses some in-depth mathematics to determine the angles and motions to handle five arms and also adjust when there are only four arms.

What does this have to do with AI self-driving cars?

At the Cybernetic Self-Driving Car Institute, we are developing self-adapting resiliency for AI self-driving cars.

Here's what we mean by self-adapting resiliency for AI self-driving cars (allow me a moment to elaborate).

Suppose a self-driving car is going along a highway and all of a sudden the left front camera that detects nearby objects happens to fail.

Now, if you are questioning why it would fail, well, it could fail simply because hardware sensory devices are going to fail from time-to-time on self-driving cars just as any other kind of hardware device can fail. It could fail due to wearing out, it could fail due to perhaps weather conditions such as especially high heat or bitter cold, it could fail because something hits it like a rock thrown up from the roadway, and so on. You might as well face the harsh truth that the hardware on self-driving cars is going to fail over time. It will happen. Right now, the self-driving cars are being pampered by the auto makers and tech firms and so you never hear about sensors failing on those cars. Besides the fact that the self-driving cars are equipped with topnotch sensors and those sensors are nearly brand new, those self-driving cars are continually getting checked and rechecked like an airplane and the crews maintaining those experimental self-driving cars try to ensure that a sensor will not end-up failing in the field.

Once we have self-driving cars owned by the public, I assure you that those self-driving cars are not going to lead such a pampered life. Most people don't take very good care of their conventional cars, including not making sure they do their oil changes regularly, and otherwise just assume their car will work until it doesn't anymore. Self-driving cars are going to be chock full of dozens and dozens of finicky sensors and you can bet that those sensors will not be well kept and will ultimately fail while the self-driving car is in motion.

Okay, with that said, let's go back to the notion that the left front camera suddenly fails while the self-driving car is rolling along a highway. We'll assume that the camera was being used to detect near-term objects (meanwhile, let's assume there are other near-term cameras on other parts of the self-driving car and also lots of other sensors such as sonar, LIDAR, radar, and the like).

What should the AI of the self-driving car do?

First, of course, it has to discover that the camera has failed. This should be a core aspect of the AI system, namely that it should be continually checking to see that the sensors are functioning. If a sensor does not respond to queries or is not providing sensor data, the AI system needs to know and needs to realize the impact of this failing sensor. Sadly, and scarily, some of the AI self-driving cars of today do not do much in the way of checking for failed sensor devices. Generally, they assume that all sensors are working all of the time, unless the sensor says otherwise.

Determining the failure of a sensor can be admittedly tricky. A sensor might be partially failing and so it is still providing data, but perhaps the data coming into the AI system is flaky. How is the AI system to realize that the data is flaky or faulty? Again, some of today's AI self-driving cars don't do any double-checking on the data coming from the sensors. There are some relatively simple ways to check and see if the data coming into the AI system from the sensor is at least "reasonable" in that it matches to what is expected to be coming from that sensor.

Some sensors are designed with their own internal error checking and so they are able to self-determine when they are faulting. This kind of capability is handy because then the device merely reports to the AI system that it is itself not working properly. If the sensor device is faulty, the question then arises whether to continue to try and make use of whatever it provides, or maybe the AI system should instead decide that the device is suspect and so reject outright whatever it sends into the sensor fusion. Imagine if the left front camera is faulty and reports that a dog is just a few feet from the heading of the self-driving car, does the AI system opt to believe the sensor and so take evasive action, or, if the AI system already suspects the device is faulty should it just ignore the data.

As you can see, these kinds of aspects about an AI self-driving car are quite crucial. It can mean life or death for those occupants in the self-driving car and for those outside of the self-driving car. A self-driving car that cannot see a dog that is to the left of the self-driving car could run right into the dog. Or, a false reporting of a dog by a suspect sensor could cause the AI to take evasive actions that cause the car to run off the road and injure the occupants (while trying to save a dog ghost).

Our viewpoint is that AI self-driving cars need to be resilient, akin to the brittle star, and be able to actively ascertain when something has gone amiss. Furthermore, besides detecting that something is amiss, the AI needs to be prepared to do something about it. For every sensor on the self-driving car, the AI needs to have in-advance a strategy about how it will handle a failure of each sensor. In short, the AI needs to be self-adapting to achieve resiliency and do so to safely keep the self-driving car and its occupants from harm, or, at least attempt to minimize harm if no other recourse is viable.

We rate the AI of self-driving cars on a five-point scale:

1. Not resilient
2. Minimally resilient
3. Moderately resilient
4. Highly resilient
5. Fully resilient

An advanced version of AI that has all the bells-and-whistles associated with resiliency, along with having been tested to show that it can actually work, earns the fully resilient top score. This requires a lot of effort and attention to go toward the resiliency factors of an AI self-driving car.

Not only does this pertain to the sensors, but it pertains to all other facets of the self-driving car. Keep in mind that a self-driving car is still a car, and therefore the AI needs to also be fully aware of whether the engine is working or faulty, whether the tires are working or faulty, whether the transmission is working or faulty, and so on. The whole kit and caboodle.

And, it even means that if the AI itself has faults, the AI needs to be aware of it and be ready to do something about it. You might question how the AI itself could become faulty, but you need to keep in mind that the AI is just software, and software will have bugs and problems, and so the AI needs to do a double-check on itself. Furthermore, the AI is running on microprocessors and using memory, all of which can have faults, and thus cause the AI system to also be faulty.

Some might say that it is impossible for the AI to be able to handle the unexpected. Suppose a tree falls down and clips the front of the self-driving car, and so now let's assume that several sensors such as some radar and cameras are faulty or completely out of commission. How could the AI have known that a tree was going to fall on the self-driving car? Plus, how it could have predicted that the tree would knock out say six sensors specifically?

Well, unless we have AI that can see the future (don't hold your breath on that one), I agree that it would not know necessarily that a tree was going to fall on the car and nor that the tree would knock out certain sensors. But, let's not think of the word "unexpected" as though it means generally being unpredictable.

The AI could have been developed with the notion that at times there will be one or more sensors that will become faulty. It could be any combination of the various sensors on the self-driving car. The fact that a tree caused those sensors to become busted is not especially material to the overall aspect that the AI should be ready to deal with six sensors that are busted. We can make a prediction that someday there will be those six sensors that fail, and do so without having to know why or how it happens.

To explore the possibilities of self-driving car failure points, we make use of a System Element Failure Matrix (SEFM), which provides a cross indication of which system elements can make-up for the loss of some other system element when it goes down. If a camera on the left that detects near-term objects is out, suppose that there is a side camera and the right-side camera that can be used to make-up for the loss of the left camera. Those two cameras, in combination with say the radar unit on the left, might still be able to deal with the same aspects that the faulty camera can no longer detect.

The AI needs to be able to ascertain what can still be done with the self-driving car, whenever any number of sensors or any other aspects of the self-driving car fails. I know that many of the self-driving car makers are saying that the self-driving car will be directed by the AI to slow down the self-driving car and pull over to the side of the road. That's a nice approach, if it is actually feasible. In some cases, the self-driving car won't be able to do such a nice idealized gradual slow down and a nice idealized pulling off to the side of the road.

Indeed, the AI needs to have Situational Action Choices (SAC), ready to go. Perhaps the AI should direct the self-driving car to actually speed-up, maybe doing so to avoid an accident that would otherwise happen if it opted to slow down. The AI must have a range of choices available, and determine based on the situation which of those choices makes the most sense to employ, including whether to use an evasive maneuver, a defensive maneuver, or whatever is applicable.

In addition, the AI needs to take time into account on whatever it does. Sometimes, a failing element on the self-driving car will go out nearly instantaneously. In other cases, the element might be gradually getting worse over time. This all implies that in some instances there will be time available due to being warned that an element is going bad, while in other cases there might be almost no reaction time available.

Furthermore, one faulty element might not be the only of the faults that are going to occur. In some cases, a faulty device might happen to fail and only it fails, while in other cases it might be sequential with several devices failing one after another, and in other cases it might be cascading of both sequential and simultaneous failures. The AI cannot be setup to assume that only a singular failure will occur. Instead, it must be ready for multiple failures, and that those failures can happen all at once or take time to appear.

How do humans deal with car failures?

Our reaction time to failures while driving a car can be on the order of several seconds, which is precious time when a car is hurling forward at seventy miles an hour or about to hit someone or something. Fortunately, the AI has the capacity to make decisions much faster than the human reaction time, but, this is only a computational advantage and one that if not readied will not necessarily arise. In other words, yes, the AI system might be able to do things in milliseconds or nanoseconds or even much faster, though it all depends on what it is trying to do. How much processing is the AI going to do to ascertain what has happened and what must be done next?

Humans often react by trying to think things through, and they are trying to mentally sort out what is happening and what to do about it. Race car drivers are trained for this kind of thinking and so are relatively well honed for it. The average car driver usually though is not well mentally prepared. They often just react by doing what seems natural, namely jamming on the brakes. Humans often get mentally confused when car elements fail and are at times mentally thrown into shock.

We don't want the AI for self-driving cars that go into "shock" and nor that are baffled by what to do when self-driving car elements falter or fail. They need to be more like the race car drivers. The AI system needs to have resiliency built into it and be able to self-adapt to whatever situation might arise.

If you've seen the movie Sully, there's a great scene in the movie where Captain Chesley Sully Sullenberger (portrayed by Tom Hanks) makes some pointed remarks about simulations of the emergency landing that he made into the Hudson River after his US Airways flight had struck birds and both jet engines flamed out. The simulations seemed to show that he could have made it safely to a nearby airport, rather than ditching the plane into the water. He points out that the simulations were made to immediately turn back to the airport the moment the birds struck the plane. This is not the way of the real world, in that he and his co-pilot had to first determine what had happened and try to then decide what to do next. This took perhaps thirty seconds to do.

I liked this scene because it brings up in my mind the importance of AI being self-adapting and resilient with respect to a self-driving car -- and that time is such a vital factor.

How much time will the AI have to figure out what has failed and what to do about it? The AI developers for self-driving cars need to push toward having the AI be able do this kind of figuring out in as fast a manner as feasible, and yet do so while still trying to determine as much as possible what has happened and what to do next.

These are aspects that it might not be able to ascertain to a certainty, and likely not due to the time crunch involved. Probabilities will be required. In a sense, "judgements" will need to be made by the AI (meaning, in this case, selecting a course of action under imperfect information about the situation). As such, the AI will need to be able to make "educated hunches" in some circumstances, lest the time required to make a "full and complete" decision would mean that the danger has gotten even worse or that there is no time left to avoid something quite untoward.

The public probably will find it disturbing to realize that AI in a self-driving had to take "shortcuts" in its processing in order to solve the problem in the time allotted, and will instead want an all-knowing AI that computes everything to an utter certainty. Don't think that's going to be the case. In whatever manner the AI does it, we must make sure that we as humans know how it did it, even if only being able to ask after-the-fact what the AI deliberated and decided to do. The auto makers and tech companies making AI self-driving cars need to consider how they will be achieving self-adapting resilient self-driving cars. I'll go for a drive in one, if it's the full resiliency level.

CHAPTER 16

PRISONER'S DILEMMA

AND

AI SELF-DRIVING CARS

CHAPTER 16

PRISONER'S DILEMMA

AND AI SELF-DRIVING CARS

When I get to work each morning, I often see a duel between car drivers when they reach the gate that goes into the workplace parking garage. Let me describe the situation for you.

For those drivers such as me that tend to come into the parking garage from a major street that runs in front of the parking facility, we turn into a narrow alley that then leads to a gate arm. You need to then take out your pass card, wave it at the panel that will open the gate, and the gate arm then rises up (assuming you have a valid card). At this juncture, you are able to drive into the parking structure. This works just fine most of the time in the sense that once the gate arm is up, you zoom ahead into the parking structure.

But, it turns out that there is a second gate that is inside the parking structure and it allows traffic that is already in the structure to get onto the same parking floor as the gate that connects to the major street. This other gate arm is directly in front of the gate that I go through. So, what sometimes happens is that the gate opens from the street side, and there is a car inside the structure that at that same moment opens the gate that is just a few feet in front of the street side gate. Now, you have two cars facing each other, both wanting to go into the parking structure, but only one can do so at a time (because of the thin neck of the parking structure where the two gates are setup).

Imagine a duel in the old west days. Two gunslingers, both with loaded guns, eyeing each other. One waits for the other since either one might suddenly spring forth with their gun. Who will pull their gun out first? The same thing happens when both gates open at the same time. One car driver eyes the other car driver. Is the other car driver going to go first, or should I go first, that's what's in the mind of each driver.

Now, there are some car drivers that seem to not care that the other car driver might suddenly go forward, and as a result, these careless or heartless drivers just move forward and take what they seem to think is their birthright to always go first. This often seems to work out, admittedly. I've never seen two cars that crashed into each other. That being said, there are situations where both of the car drivers at each of the gates seems to believe they each have a birthright to make the first move. And, in those instances, the two cars have gotten pretty close to hitting each other. Typically, in this instance, they get within inches, one opts to stop, and the other driver zips ahead.

There are also the nervous nellies, or maybe they should more properly be known as courteous drivers, for whom when the gates open, each of those type of car driver looks to the other driver to go ahead and make the first move. These car drivers are willing to give the other driver the right of way. This is pretty nice, except admittedly sometimes it means that both cars are sitting there, waiting for the other, and because they are so giving that they are apparently willing to sit there forever (it seems), and meanwhile the car drivers behind them get really ticked off. You see, the gate arms are up, and yet nobody is moving, which can anger other drivers. If you are someone that is nearly late for work, and you see that nobody is moving, and yet the gate arms are up, you would be quite upset that you are being held back and that no one is moving ahead.

I've spoken with many of these drivers of each kind. The ones that are the birthright believers would say that it isn't necessarily that they think they have a right of way, but instead they insist that their method is the most efficient. By not waiting around, they are moving the lines forward. Their belief is that all drivers should always be moving ahead as soon as the gate arm opens. If this means that you might also make contact with another car, that's fine, since it is the modest cost for keeping the line moving efficiently. These car drivers also think that the ones that wait once the gate opens are idiots, they are stupid because they are holding up the line and making things be inefficient.

The ones that are willing to wait for the other driver believe that this is the right way to do things. They believe it minimizes the potential for crashing into other cars. It is polite. It is civilized. The other car drivers that insist on the right of way are piggish. Those piggish drivers don't care about other people and are ego-centric. They are the ones that ruin the world for everyone else.

Which is right and which is wrong?

You tell me. I'm not sure we can definitely call either one always right or always wrong. Certainly, the ones that increase the risk of cars hitting each other are endangering the lives of others, and so we could likely ascribe they are wrong for taking that first move. I suppose though that those drivers would say that you might have drivers coming into the line that might hit the other cars ahead of them, since once the gate arm opens it suggests everyone should be moving forward, and so maybe there is that risk that needs to be compared to the risk of two cars hitting each other once the gates are open and the two cars are facing off.

It's a conundrum, for sure.

Some of you might recognize this problem as one that has been affectionately called the Prisoner's Dilemma.

In the case of the prisoner's dilemma, you are to pretend that there are two people that have been arrested and are being held by the police in separate rooms. The two have no means to communicate with each other. They were each potentially involved in the same crime. A prosecutor is willing to offer them each a deal.

The deal is that if one of them betrays the other and says that the other one did the crime, the one that does the betraying will be set free if the other one has remained silent (and in that case the other one will get 3 years in jail). But, if the other one has also tried to betray the one that is doing the betraying, they will both get 2 years in jail. If neither of them betrays the other, they will each get 1 year in jail.

So, if you were one of those prisoners, what would you do?

Would you betray the other one, doing so in hopes that the other one remains silent and so you can then go free? Of course, if the other one also betrays you, you both are going to jail for 2 years. Even worse, if you have remained silent and the other one betrays you, you'll go to jail for 3 years. You could pin your hopes on the other one remaining silent and you opt to remain silent, figuring in that case you both only get 1 year each.

Another conundrum, for sure!

If you were to create a so-called payoff matrix, you would put on one axis the choices for you, and on the other axis the choices for the other person. You would have a 2x2 matrix, consisting of you remaining silent, you betraying the other, on one axis, and the other axis would have the other person remaining silent, or betraying you.

There is the viewpoint that by remaining silent you are trying to cooperate with the other person, while if you betray the other person then you are essentially defecting from cooperating. If you defect and the other person tries to cooperate, you get the payoff temptation labeled as T. If you cooperate and the other person cooperates, you get the payoff reward labeled as R. If you defect and the other person defects then you get the payoff punishment labeled as P. If you cooperate and the other person defect, you get the payoff "sucker bet" labeled as S.

In the game as I've described it: $T > R > P > S$

I mention this because there are numerous variations of the dilemma in terms of the amount of payoff involved for each of the four choices, and it makes a difference in that unless the above is true, namely $T > R$, $R > P$, $P > S$, then the logic about what choice you should logically make is changed.

Anyway, what would you do? In theory, you are better off with betraying the other prisoner. This would be a proper thing to do in a rational self-interested way, since it offers the greatest option for the least of the penalties that you might get.

Now, you might try to fight the problem by saying that it depends on the nature of the other person. You might think that certainly you would already know the other fellow prisoner and so you would already have an inkling of how the other person is going to vote. If you knew that the other person was the type to remain silent, then you would indeed want to remain silent. If you knew that the other person was the type to fink on others, you'd presumably want to betray them.

But, we are going to say that you don't know the other person and do not know what choice they are likely or unlikely to make. Going back to the car drivers at the open gates, the car driver looking at the other car driver does not know that other person and does not know if they are the type of person that will zoom ahead or will be willing to wait. It's the same kind of situation. Complete strangers that do not know what the other one will do.

You might feel better about the world if I were to tell you that humans in these kinds of games have tended toward cooperative behavior and would more than not be willing to assume that the other person will act cooperatively too. I hope that boosts your feelings about humanity. Well, keep in mind that those that aren't the cooperative types are now thinking that you are sheep and they like the idea that there are lots of sheep in the world. Sorry.

You might somewhat object to this prisoner's dilemma since it only is a one-time deal. You might wonder what would someone do if the same dilemma happened over and over. There is indeed the iterative prisoner's dilemma, in which you play the game once, then after the outcome is known, you play it again, and so on. This makes for a quite different situation. You now can see what your other prisoner is doing over time, and opt to respond based on what the other person does.

When the number of times that the play is iterated is known to the players, the proper rational thing to do is for each to betray. In that sense, it is just like the single-shot game play. On the other hand, if the number of iterations is unknown, it is a toss-up as to whether to cooperate or to defect.

For the multiple plays, there are various strategies you can use. One is the "nice person" strategy of starting as a cooperative person and only switching if the other does a betray. The extreme of the nice person strategy is to always cooperate no matter what, but usually the other person will realize this and will then switch to betray for the rest of the game.

You might find of interest that these prisoner dilemma games have been played in numerous tournaments. One of the most winning strategies was done in four lines of programming code and became known as tit-for-tat. Whatever the other person did, the program did the same thing on the next move. The only problem here is that often the game then goes into a death spiral of both players always defecting. As such, there is a variant that is tit-for-tat with some forgiveness, which will detect if a certain number of continuous betrayals has occurred and will then switch to cooperate in hopes that the other side will do so too.

What does this have to do with AI self-driving cars?

At the Cybernetic Self-Driving Car Institute, we are developing AI for self-driving cars and there will be instances when a self-driving car will need to make these kinds of prisoner dilemma decisions, such as the case of the open gates and deciding who goes first.

You've likely heard about the famous example of the self-driving car that came to a four-way stop sign and waited for the other cars to go ahead, which it did because the other cars were driven by humans and those humans realized that if they rolled through the stop sign they could intimidate the self-driving car. The AI of the self-driving car had been developed to avoid potentially leading to a crash and so it sat at the stop sign waiting for the other cars to give it a turn to go.

If we had only self-driving cars on the roadways, presumably they would have each neatly stopped at the stop sign, and then would have abided by the usual rule of the first one there goes, or that the one to the right goes, or something like that. There would not have been a stand-off. They might even be able to communicate with each other via a local V2V (vehicle to vehicle communication system).

But, we are going to have a mixture of both human driven cars and AI driven self-driving cars for many years, if not even forever, and so the AI of the self-driving car cannot assume that the other cars are being driven by AI. The AI needs to know how to deal with human drivers.

Suppose your self-driving car is on the freeway and a car in the next lane signals that it wants into the lane of the self-driving car. Should it let the other car in? If the AI does this, it could be that pushy human drivers realize that the AI is a sucker, and the next thing you know all the other cars around the self-driving car are trying to also cut into the lane. At some point, the AI needs to know when to allow someone else in and when not to do so.

If the AI is playing the always cooperate mode, it will be just like the prisoner's dilemma that others will do the betray always to the AI because they know that the AI will cave in. Don't think we want that.

In fact, there might be some owners of self-driving cars that will insist they want their self-driving car AI to be the betraying type. Just as they themselves are perhaps that ego-centric person, they might want that their self-driving car has the same kind of dominant approach to driving. You might be thinking that we don't need to let such car owners have their way, and that maybe the auto makers should make all self-driving cars be the cooperating type. Or, maybe we should have federal and state regulations that say an AI cannot be the betraying type and so this will force all AI to be the same way. Again, this is highly questionable and raises the same points made earlier about the mix of human drivers and AI drivers.

I realize you might find it shocking to think that the AI would be potentially a pushy driver and insist on getting its way. Imagine a human driver that encounters such a self-centered self-driving car. Will the human driver have road rage against the AI self-driving car? No darned machine is going to take cuts in front of me, you can just hear the human driver screaming in anger. Fortunately, we are unlikely to get any road rage from the AI when the human cuts it off while driving, though, if we train the AI by the way that humans drive, it could very well have a hidden and embedded road rage within its deep learning neural network.

The ability to discern what to do in the prisoner's dilemma circumstances is a needed skill for the AI of any self-driving car that is seeking to be a Level 5 (a Level 5 is a true self-driving car that can do whatever a human driver can do). Besides providing that type of AI skill, the other aspect is whether to allow the self-driving car owner or human occupant to modify what it is. For example, the voice command system of the AI in the self-driving car could interact with the owner or occupant and find out which dominant strategy to use, allowing the human owner or occupant to select whatever they prefer in the situation. If you are late for work, maybe you go with the betray, while if you are on leisurely drive and in no rush then maybe you choose the cooperative. Or, maybe the AI needs to ascertain the type of person you are, and take on your personality. It's a tough driving world out there and the tit-for-tat is just one of many ways to for your AI to make its way through the world.

CHAPTER 17
TURING TEST
AND
AI SELF-DRIVING CARS

CHAPTER 17

TURING TEST
AND AI SELF-DRIVING CARS

When my children were young, I used to teach them various games such as checkers, chess, Monopoly, and other such fun pastimes. In doing so, I would watch in apt fascination as they played these various games. I was interested in how they played the games and how much further they could go beyond whatever rudimentary tactics and strategies I might have shown them. It was intriguing to gauge how much cognitive capability they had to extend their initial learning and then develop their own expanded strategies and tactics in the games.

As I watched them make moves in the games, let's take chess as an example, at first I could see them making all of the simplest foundation moves, along with seeing their gambits in trying to tie together several moves into a larger tactic or strategy. When I saw one of them play against another child of their same age, I realized that by watching the chess moves I could pretty quickly estimate the age of the child and whether indeed a child was playing versus an adult playing the game.

I could even detect whether the game was being played by my own son or daughter, due to my having gotten used to their line of play in chess. In other words, even if I could not see who was playing the chess game, if you gave me a list of the moves made by each participant, I could tell you which one was my son or daughter and which one was someone else. If you tried to trick me and gave me a list of game moves in which my son or daughter were not playing in the game, I could even pretty reliably say that they weren't playing the game and that none of the players was them.

Of course, as they got older, the nature of their game playing became more sophisticated and it became harder too to recognize their specific style or approach. It also would take longer and longer game plays for me to try and figure out who was who. Before, I could immediately discern by the opening moves as to who was whom. But, as my children grew more complex in their thinking and their game playing, it was increasingly hard to spot their own style and it would at times only be after much of the game was played that I could make an educated guess about whom the player was.

Recently, researchers at the Universite de Toulouse and the Universite Paris-Saclay conducted an interesting study of play in the the game Go. You likely are aware that the game of Go has become a great fascination for AI as it is a game that has complexities that differ from chess and make it a lively source of insight as to how to program to play games. Some had made predictions that it would be a long time before AI could play as well as the top rated human Go players. But, in 2017, the Google AI Go playing software called AlphaGo beat the world's top ranked player at the time, and the software was granted a 9-dan ranking.

The researchers at Toulouse and Paris-Saclay were curious about how the game of Go were being played. They wanted to study the game moves made by the players, including both the human players and the computer AI playing software packages. Remember how I mentioned earlier that when my children played chess that I could recognize it was them by the moves they made in the game? Well, the question arose by these university researchers as to whether one could discern a human player from an AI system player by the nature of their moves made.

What do you think they discovered?

Let me tell you what they did and what they found out. They first put together databases of Go game playing. They collected 8,000 Go game instances played by humans, 8,000 games played by a software package called Gnugo (known for using a deterministic game playing approach), 8,000 games played by a software package called Fuego (known for using a Monte Carlo approach), and 50 games that were played by the top AI winner AlphaGo. From these games, the researchers prepared a weighted directed network graph to be able to aid in identifying patterns of play.

They found that some of the networks had hubs or communities, essentially areas of the network that had a dense set of incoming and outgoing links (their mathematical metrics are elaborated in their paper "Distinguishing Humans from Computers in the Game of Go: A Complex Network Approach" by Coquide, Georgeot, and Giraud). In their analysis, they found that these hubs or communities were somewhat readily and frequently within the network graphs of the computer playing systems moves, plus these communities seemed to be weakly linked to other areas of the network. Meanwhile, in contrast, the human players appeared to have fewer such communities in their sets of moves, and interestingly the communities tended to strongly link with other areas of the network (in contrast to how the computer playing systems played).

In short, the researchers contend that via this telltale sign, a kind of signature is seen, and it would be possible to presumably distinguish between whether a computer system was a player versus whether a human was a player. We might quibble with their claim of being able to make such a distinction due to their sample size of the number of games played might seem somewhat smaller than might be otherwise more convincing if they had a much larger analysis set. Also, one might wonder whether the play characteristics of the computer players might change over time, in the sense that maybe this is just an initial evolution of AI playing of Go and that with more advancements made in the AI playing that it might begin to have a pattern more akin to the human pattern.

Anyway, the researchers opted to comment even further outside-of-the-box and proposed an interesting idea. They suggested that it might be feasible to consider a form of the Turing Test that would involve game play and then use the moves to try and ascertain which player was a human and which was the computer. If you aren't familiar with the Turing Test, allow me a moment to share with you what that's all about, and also why then this out-of-the-box thinking is kind of interesting.

The Turing Test was named after the famous mathematician Alan Turing, whom you've likely heard of in your math classes or maybe you've seen some of the movies and documentaries made about his life. In 1950, he wrote a paper that was about the topic of how we could discern whether or not computers can think. He suggested that rather than getting mired in what "thinking" is (in other words, you would first need to define the nature of thinking to be able to say whether something does it or not), he postulated that maybe we could construct a test that would illustrate presumably whether someone or something was able to think.

The test is rather simple to describe. Imagine that you had a human behind one door, and an AI system behind another door, and then another human stood outside the two doors and asked questions of the two that are hidden behind the respective doors. The questions would be passed back-and-forth in writing and thus eliminate the chance of guessing which one was the human and which was the AI by just the mere act of communicating with the player. In those days, when Turing wrote the research paper, they didn't have texting like we do now, and so it is obviously much easier these days to envision such a test than it would have been logistically arranged in the 1950's (the computer would have been a gigantic hardware system that today is comparable to a typical hand-sized smartphone).

The interrogator then asks questions of each of the two players and eventually, presumably, the interrogator either is able to discern which is the computer -- or, cannot tell the difference between the two players and therefore the computer is considered equivalent to the human player. In the case of the computer being undistinguishable from the human player, the computer has passed the Turing Test and succeeded in (apparently) demonstrating that it is a thinking system since it equaled a thinking human. Notice that this then avoids the whole issue of what is "thinking" because in this case the test is solely about whether the AI can do as well as a human that thinks, and thus we have no need to understand how thinking actually operates.

The Turing Test is a frequently mentioned item in the AI field and even outside of the AI field. It has become a kind of legendary icon that many refer to, though many aren't actually aware of what its downsides are.

Let's cover some of those downsides.

One obvious concern is that the human being used in the Turing Test as a player must be intelligent enough that we would grant that they are able to appropriately play this game. In other words, if we placed a nitwit behind one of the doors and they were mentally out of it, we would be hard pressed to say that just because the AI matched the human that it means that the AI really has shown itself to be intelligent per se.

An equal concern is the nature of the interrogator. If the interrogator does not know what they are doing, they might be asking questions that aren't very good to help probe for intelligence per se. Imagine that the interrogator asks the two to tell how they feel. One says it feels really good and happy, while the other says that it feels sad and downtrodden. Tell me, which of the two is the human and which is the AI? You can't know.

I had one smart aleck tell me that they would ask each to calculate pi to a million digits, and whichever of the two could give the answer it must be the computer. Sigh. I pointed out that the human might have a computer with them (we've not said that they cannot) and might use it to help determine the calculation. Or, maybe the AI could calculate it, but has been programmed not to fall for such a silly trap and will pretend that it cannot calculate the result, and thus presumably be as unable to do so as an unaided human. If both players then indicated they could not calculate pi to a million digits, could you conclude that the computer was undistinguishable from the human player? I think not.

There is a slew of other problems associated with the Turing Test as a type of test for discerning whether a computer might be considered a thinking thing. Won't go into those other downsides here, but I just caution you to be mindful of not blindly believing that the Turing Test is going to one day soon allow us to declare that AI has finally arrived. The nature of the test to do so, whichever test we all decide to use, needs to be rigorous enough that we would all feel confident in what the test actually reveals.

Now, back to the point about the researchers that claim they can distinguish between humans and computers in the playing of Go. Their added interesting idea was that maybe for the Turing Test we could dispense with asking questions of the two players, and instead have them play a game, such as Go. We could then analyze their game play afterward, and if we could not see a statistically significant difference in their game play we might then suggest that the computer has passed this modified version of the Turing Test.

Of course, this modified version of the Turing Test is not much better than the original Turing Test. For example, we need to decide what game is going to be played. Is Go an appropriate game? Maybe some other game instead? But, either way, just because a game can be played is not much of a wide enough swath of the nature of intelligence as we know it. In other words, does the ability to play a game, whether it be Go or chess or whatever, really embody the full range of aspects that we consider involving thinking? I don't think it does, and I am guessing you agree with me.

I do though applaud the researchers for bringing up the idea. It points out that maybe it's not the questions themselves that are the only focus of a Turing Test, but also the nature of how someone responds over time, in the same sense that the moves in a game showcase presumably some kind of "thinking" without having to probe directly into what thinking is.

What does this have to do with AI self-driving cars?

Glad you asked!

At the Cybernetic Self-Driving Car Institute, we are keenly interested in and we are pursuing how we all will be able to agree that an AI self-driving car has achieved the vaunted Level 5.

By the word "all" here, we mean that AI researchers, government officials, auto makers, the general public, and basically everyone would be able to agree when a self-driving car has earned a Level 5 badge of honor.

In the standard definition for the levels of AI self-driving cars, the Level 5 is the topmost level and means that a self-driving car is driven by the AI in whatever manner that a human could drive a car. On the surface of things, maybe this seems like an airtight way to describe the Level 5. Unfortunately, it is not.

Suppose I have developed a self-driving car and I place it into a parking lot that I have purposely built and shaped (putting special markers on the roadway, putting handy barriers around the perimeter, etc.). I have a human drive the self-driving car, and watch as the human parks the car, maneuvers in and around the parking spots, and so on. We then make the human become a passenger, or maybe even remove the human from the car, and we have the AI try to do the same things that the human did.

If the AI is able to drive the self-driving car in the same manner that the human did, can we declare that this self-driving car is a Level 5?

You might say, yes, indeed it is a Level 5 because it drove as a human would. Really? That's all we need to do to achieve a Level 5?

Notice that we severely constrained the driving environment. It is a confined space with specialized markings to make life easier for the AI system. Also, there wasn't much driving needed per se in the constrained space. You couldn't go faster than maybe 10-15 miles per hour. You didn't need to avoid obstacles because we made sure the parking lot was pristine. And on, and on.

Do you still believe that this self-driving car merits a Level 5? I would contend that we can't really say from such a limited test that the self-driving car fulfills the true sense of what we all seem to be thinking is a Level 5 self-driving car. If you are willing to say this is a Level 5 then you would presumably be willing to say that the cars on a

Disneyland ride are also at a Level 5 because they can do whatever a human can do when driving those cars.

In a sense, we need a better way to test whether a self-driving car is a true Level 5 – you might say we need a type of Turing Test.

Could we just use the Turing Test as is? Not really. The Turing Test is aimed towards general intelligence, while the task of driving a car is more of a limited scope form of intelligence. We can though borrow from the Turing Test and say that if we want to test a self-driving car we should have some form of interrogatives about driving and some kind of judge or judges to be able to decide whether the self-driving car has achieved a Level 5.

We need to have an open-ended kind of test in that if we were to reveal beforehand all of the test aspects, perhaps a clever developer could try to prepare the AI to pass that particular test, but that it still would not be what we seem to intend, namely that the AI must be able to drive the car in whatever manner a human could drive a car.

Speaking of which, when we say that a human could drive a car, are we referring to a novice driver that has just taken a beginner's class in driving, or are we referring to the average adult driver, or maybe are we referring to a race car driver? The nature of the comparison is crucial, just as we pointed out in the case of the Turing Test that the human behind the door must be someone we would agree is a thinking being of intelligence, otherwise we won't have a suitable basis for comparison.

Some say to me that we're getting overly complicated and that if an AI self-driving car is able to drive around a neighborhood without being aided by a human that it certainly has achieved a Level 5. Any typical neighborhood is okay by these pundits, as they claim that a typical location with pedestrians, dogs, potholes, and the rest is enough. I then ask them about freeways – shouldn't a Level 5 self-driving car be able to do that too? What about the weather conditions, such as if it is a sunny day versus a snowing day with ice on the roads?

And, how long does the test need to be? If the self-driving car can successfully drive around for let's say 10 minutes, is that enough time to have "proven" what it can do? I doubt any of us would think such a short time is sufficient. Also, suppose the self-driving car drives around for 5 hours, but does not encounter a child that runs out into the street. Wouldn't we want to know that the AI is able to handle that kind of circumstance?

Some believe that we should have a detailed list of the myriad of driving situations and that we could use that list to test whether a self-driving car is really a Level 5. This might be better than no test, and better than a test that is simplistic, and so it does help get us somewhat towards being able to agree as to a Level 5 when we see it.

Keep in mind that we're not getting bogged down in semantics about whether something can be labeled as a Level 5. The Level 5 is an important marker for progress in the field of self-driving cars. It is the ultimate goal for all self-driving car makers that want to achieve a true self-driving car. The issue is that we might not know when we have gotten there. Without some agreed substantive means to test for it, we'll likely have false claims that it has been achieved. This will confuse and confound all, including other AI developers, government regulators, the general public, and others. Let's all work together on a Turing Test for self-driving cars, and whomever comes up with it we might agree we'll name it after that person (your chance for immortality!).

CHAPTER 18

SUPPORT VECTOR

MACHINES

FO AI SELF-DRIVING CARS

CHAPTER 18
SUPPORT VECTOR MACHINES
FOR AI SELF-DRIVING CARS

I am very active in my alma mater. I serve on several alumni boards and committees, and try to support the youth of today that will soon be the inventers and innovators of tomorrow. As a mentor for our campus start-up incubator, it is exciting and refreshing to see so many entrepreneurs that are desirous of launching the next Facebook or Google. Hurrah for them and let's all hope that they keep their spirits high and remain determined in their quest.

Since I just said hurrah, it reminds me of cheering, and cheering reminds me of sports, so perhaps it would be timely for me to mention that I also enjoy going to our exciting football games and our boisterous basketball games. Our football team is generally more highly ranked than our basketball team, but either way, whether we win or lose, it's fun to be a supportive alumnus that cheers on his teams.

Which brings up a question for you. Let's suppose that we recently managed to snag an incoming student that will be a great addition to our football team, and another student that will be a superb addition to our basketball team. The two students we'll say are named A and B. I'd like you to try and guess which went to which of our two sports teams.

The student A is 6 foot 2 inches tall and weighs about 260 pounds.

The student B is 6 foot 8 inches tall and weighs about 220 pounds.

- Did A go to the football team or the basketball team?

- Did B go to the football team or the basketball team?

You might at first glance say that there's no way to tell which went to which. I didn't provide enough information such as how high each can jump and nor whether one of them made a ton of touchdowns last year. But, I did give you some info that would be helpful, namely, their height and weight.

By now, I assume that you have deduced that A went to the football team, while B went to the basketball team. This seems logical since B is rather tall and we'd expect a basketball player to be relatively tall. A is shorter than B, and a bit heavier, which makes sense for a football player.

You used your awareness of the physical characteristics normally required for each of those two sports to try and figure out the most likely classification that matched to the description of A and that matched to the description of B. Sure, you could still be wrong and maybe the football team wanted a really tall football player to block kicks, and maybe the shorter of the two would be really wily and fast on a basketball court, but by-and-large you made a pretty reasonable guess that A should be tossed into the football classification and that B should be put into the basketball classification.

Congratulations, as you are now a Support Vector Machine (SVM).

Well, kind of. Allow me a moment to explain what a Support Vector Machine is.

SVM is a statistical method that aids in classifying things. You typically feed various training examples into the SVM mathematical algorithm, and it tries to identify how to best classify the data. As an example, I might have data about football players and basketball players, let's say their height and weight, and I enter that into a SVM. The algorithm analyzes the data tries to come up with a mathematical classification for the two.

Henceforth, if you were to have an A or B come along (two sports players), it could try to tell you into which classification each belongs.

Notice that I mentioned that we provided the SVM with training data. We had two classes, namely football players and basketball players. The training data consisted of data points, in this case suppose I had data describing one hundred football players and one hundred basketball players, and so I provided two hundred instances and gave the height and weight for each of those instances. These data points could be considered a p-dimensional vector, and the SVM develops a p-1 dimensional hyperplane that has the largest separation or margin between the two classes.

The hyperplane is essentially a means to divide the two classes from each other. It is a mathematical construct that aims to ensure that the widest separation between the two classes is found. In this manner, when a new data point comes along, such as our student A, the algorithm can look to see if A is in the football classification or on the other side of the hyperplane and actually in the basketball classification. It's kind of like having a dividing wall between the two classes, and can be used to decide whether a new data point is on one side or the other side of the wall. This is formally called the maximum-margin hyperplane.

I'll add some more jargon into this.

The SVM is known as a non-probabilistic binary linear classifier.

The "binary" part means that it usually determines whether something is in a class or not, or whether it is in one of two classes. So, we have our example already of using SVM to determine whether someone is in one of two classes (football versus basketball).

We could also have used the SVM by providing only say football players (just one class), and then asked the algorithm to indicate whether someone seemed to fit into the football player classification or not. For our purposes, this would have indicated that A was in the football player class. But, for B, it would only have indicated that B was not in the football class, and would not have known anything about the basketball class, so we only would have known that it seemed that B was not in the football classification.

SVM is usually "non-probabilistic" meaning that we won't get a probability about the odds that the algorithm is correct that A is a football player and that B is a basketball player. There are special versions of SVM that do add a probabilistic capability.

SVM is usually "linear" which is the easier and straightforward way to find the hyperplane. There is a more advanced version of SVM that provides for a non-linear approach, often using something referred to as a kernel trick. This can be handy if your data points aren't amenable to the easier linear approach.

The SVM is mainly used with training examples, and therefore it is considered a "supervised" learning model. The supervision aspect is that we are providing known examples and thus giving direct guidance to the SVM as to data points and into which classes they are supposed to fit into.

Suppose though that we weren't sure of what the classifications should be.

If we had two hundred sports players and fed in the examples, but didn't say that they belonged into a football classification and/or a basketball classification, we might instead want the SVM to come up with whatever classifications it might find. We could then look at how the data had been classified by the SVM, and try to ascribe some logical basis to the mathematical classes that it found. It could be that we'd say that the classes were for football and basketball, or we might decide the classes are for something else instead.

This would then be considered an unsupervised learning model, and the SVM tries to find a "naturally occurring" way to group or classify the data. Since this is quite a bit different from the traditional SVM, the unsupervised version is often referred to as Support Vector Clustering rather than being called a Support Vector Machine.

SVM's have been used quite successfully in a variety of disciplines, such as in the biochemical sciences it has been utilized for classifying proteins. Another area that SVM is especially known for aiding is the classification of images. Suppose you had hundreds or thousands of pictures of lions and of elephants. You could feed those images into SVM and have it identify a mathematical categorization for the lions and for the elephants, and then when a new image comes along it could be fed into the SVM to have it indicate whether the image is in the lion category or in the elephant category.

What does this have to do with AI self-driving cars?

At the Cybernetic Self-Driving Car Institute, we are using SVM as an integral part of the AI self-driving car software that we are developing.

Indeed, anyone doing AI self-driving car development should be either using SVM or at least considering whether and when to use SVM. Generally, in AI, overall, the use of SVM is considered an important tool in the toolkit of AI learning models.

How does SVM get involved in AI self-driving cars, you might ask.

Suppose a self-driving car has a camera that is able to capture images of what's ahead of the self-driving car. The AI of the self-driving car might want to know whether there is a vehicle up ahead, and could feed the image into a SVM that's been trained on what vehicles look like. The SVM could do its mathematical analysis and report back to the AI system that the image does contain a vehicle or does not contain a vehicle. The AI system then can use this result, doing so in combination with other sensors and whatever those sensors are capturing such as radar signals, LIDAR images, etc.

You might be aware of AI sufficiently to wonder why the image analysis wasn't being done by a neural network. Well, you are right that usually we would be using a neural network to do the image analysis. But, suppose that we also thought it prudent to use SVM.

In essence, you can use SVM to do an initial analysis, and then do a double-check with say a trained neural network. Or, you could have used the neural network as the first analysis, and then use a SVM as a double-check on the neural network. This kind of double-checking can be quite useful, and some might argue is even a necessity.

Why would it be considered a necessity?

Suppose the neural network was our only image analyzer on the AI self-driving car. Suppose further that the neural network got confused and thought there was a vehicle in the image, but there really wasn't. Or, suppose the neural network thought there was not a vehicle in the image, but there really was. Either way, the AI of the self-driving car could be horribly misled and make a maneuver based on a mistaken analysis by the neural network. If the SVM was acting as a double-check, the AI could then consider the result from the SVM and also consult the result from the neural network, and decide what to do if the two different image analyzers had two different interpretations of what the image contains.

Thus, you can use SVM for AI self-driving cars as:

- Standalone SVM
- SVM as initial analysis, double-checked by some other approach
- SVM as a double-check upon some other approach which has been first used

You might be wondering whether the computational processing time of using the SVM might be prohibitive to use it for an AI self-driving car. Whatever AI learning models are used on a self-driving car need to be fast enough to deal with the real-time needs of guiding a self-driving car. The self-driving car might be going 70 miles per hour, and so the sensory analyses need to be fast enough to make sure that the AI gets informed in time to make prudent decisions about controlling the car.

SVM is pretty quick after having been trained, and so it is a suitable candidate for use on a self-driving car. That being said, if you want to also do further training of the SVM while it is immersed in the AI of the self-driving car, you'd need to be cautious in doing the training while the self-driving car is otherwise involved in maneuvering in traffic.

We use any non-traffic non-transportation time of the self-driving car (such as when it is parked), in order to have the SVM do additional training. Furthermore, you can push the SVM training off into the cloud, in the sense that the self-driving car if connected to a cloud-based over-the-air updating system can have SVM updates occur elsewhere so as to not bog down the self-driving car processing per se. Once the SVM has been updated in the cloud, it can be pushed back down into the local AI system of the self-driving car.

Besides doing vehicle versus non-vehicle image analysis classifications, an SVM can be used for a wide array of other aspects on an AI self-driving car. We've found it especially handy for doing pedestrian classifications. For example, whether an image contains a pedestrian or does not contain pedestrian. Even more involved would be a classification of whether a pedestrian poses a "threat" to the self-driving car or does not pose a threat. By the use of the word "threat" we mean that the pedestrian might be darting into the street in front of the self-driving car. This constitutes a form of threat in that the self-driving car might need to take some radical evasive maneuver to try and avoid hitting the pedestrian.

How would the classifier realize whether a pedestrian is a threat or not?

We train the SVM on images of pedestrians. In one set, we had pictures of pedestrians that are in a standing posture or otherwise in a posture that does not suggest dramatic movement. A stance of a pedestrian that suggests they are running would be considered a more dramatic movement. The distance of the pedestrian is another factor, since someone might be in a running posture but so far away from the self-driving car that it is not considered an imminent threat. On the other hand, if the image shows a pedestrian in a running stance that is very near to the self-driving car, the AI would want to know to be on the alert.

One of the budding areas of self-driving car capabilities involves being able to discern the intent of pedestrians. Right now, most of the AI systems for self-driving cars merely detect whether a pedestrian exists somewhere within a near virtual bubble of the self-driving car. The latest advances go further and try to guess what the intent of the pedestrian might be. Is the pedestrian moving toward the self-driving car or away from it? Are they going to end-up in front of the self-driving car or behind it? Do they seem to be looking at the self-driving car or looking elsewhere? All of these aspects help to try and gauge the intent of the pedestrian. Us human drivers are continually scanning around us, looking at pedestrians and trying to guess what the pedestrian is going to do. That's what the AI of the self-driving car should also be doing.

With an SVM, the AI needs to be cautious about being possibly led down a primrose path, so to speak. The SVM might say that something is classified as X, but it could be a false positive. For our earlier example about the sports players, suppose that the SVM had indicated that B was a football player. That's a false positive. Suppose the SVM had indicated that A was not a football player. That's a false negative. The AI of the self-driving car needs to consider whether to believe the SVM classifier, which will depend on a variety of facets, such as in the case of images whether the image is a clear image or a noisy image, and so on.

For SVM, it is wise to be cautious of the SVM results whenever the target classes tend to be very close to each other or even overlap. I am guessing that if we tried to train a SVM on baseball players and soccer players, we might find that based on height and weight alone that the two classifications are very close to each other. This means that when we have a sports player C that presents themselves to us, and if we ask the SVM to classify them, our belief in whether the SVM says that C is a baseball player or is a soccer player will need to be carefully reviewed or double-checked.

The SVM can also inadvertently overfit to the training data. Overfitting is a common problem in most learning models, including neural networks. The aspect of overfitting means that the learning becomes overly fixated on the training data and has not been able to generalize beyond the training data. Imagine a baby that is learning about blocks. Suppose the baby is given a bunch of blocks and they are all the color green and are one inch square in size. The baby might believe that all blocks are green, and can only be green, and must be one inch square in size. If you handed the baby a new block which was red, the baby might not realize it is a block. That's overfitting.

Another issue for SVM involves outliers. Suppose we happen to find a really great football player that is nearly seven feet tall. If we had included just one such instance in our training set, the SVM might have considered the outlier as irrelevant and ignored it. This could be okay, or it might be bad in that maybe we really could have football players of that size. Thus, the SVM might make a mistake that when we later on do look at a football player of that height, the SVM will instead insist that the player must be a basketball player.

So, the SVM, like other learning models, must be taken with a grain of salt. It can be prone to overfitting to the training data. It can be computational costly to do the training. It can have difficulty with outliers. It assumes that the characteristics or features being used are generally relevant to the classification. And so on.

I don't want you to though feel like I am saying don't use SVM. I assure you that any learning model, including neural networks, will have the same kinds of limitations and issues that need to be considered. The SVM is a very valuable tool in the AI toolkit and one that we believe deserves due attention for AI self-driving cars.

CHAPTER 19
EXPERT SYSTEMS
AND AI SELF-DRIVING CARS
BY
MICHAEL ELIOT

CHAPTER 19
EXPERT SYSTEMS
AND AI SELF-DRIVING CARS
BY MICHAEL ELIOT

I'd like to introduce you to the AI-specialty of Expert Systems and then provide key indicators of how Expert Systems are pertinent to AI self-driving cars.

First, we must ask ourselves what an expert system is. Often considered one of the forerunners to modern day AI, an expert system is computer software that attempts to mimic the decision-making expertise of an expert in a given field. In the past, this typically meant creating interrelated tree structures to represent decision models. Now, with the advent of machine learning, neural networks, and more advanced AI, expert systems have entered a whole new level of capability that they had not previously exhibited.

Developing an expert-oriented system is in many respects at the root of the self-driving car field, and presents many challenges. Let's take a close look at some of the key problems involved in developing an expert system for this particular domain (i.e., driving a car), and then examine a few of the important methods that are currently being used to solve these problems.

In the context of this domain, what do we mean by an "expert" when it comes to car driving. Is your average adult driver on-the-road able to be considered an expert at what they do? I've driven through enough of the harried and congested Los Angeles traffic to veto that idea. What about a professional car driver, including the likes of a race car driver, a bus driver, or a truck driver? Possibly, but race car drivers don't accurately depict the capabilities of everyway drivers, and the bus driver and truck driver don't really equate to the same expertise of a race car driver.

Perhaps we can circumvent the need for a defined expert per se by simply understanding the necessary outputs. While this seems straightforward, this becomes problematic for two reasons. First, what are the outputs being referenced? If the outputs are generated by a human driver, you simply have the same problem as the previous points about race car drivers, bus drivers, and truck drivers. If they are a derived set of desired outputs then how do you know that this is considered the optimal decision, and how do you generate the data accordingly? The second point involves determining how you equate those desired outputs with a given set of inputs. Driving is a dynamically changing environment, so you can't easily define a finite stated set of outputs for a set of inputs in all situations.

This point is a significant problem in the self-driving car world and brings us to an area of AI that is known as fuzzy decision making or more commonly fuzzy logic. Fuzzy logic has to do with deriving outputs based on probabilities and approximation, rather than using traditional non-probabilistic logical methods. Fuzzy logic is the "human" factor in expert systems. It is those gut feelings and hunches that separate the amateur from the expert, and for software engineers this can be quite difficult to identify and codify into a system. How does one code a gut feeling? One could utilize probability as an attempt to do so, but, when the life of the passenger in a self-driving car is on the line, is it safe to essentially guess at an answer? However we get there, adding in the human element of hunches and intuition is crucial to achieve a Level 4 or Level 5 self-driving car, and it is an extremely difficult aspect to pin down.

These questions are at the heart of all expert systems, and can help us articulate the challenges faced with self-driving cars. As recap, we've emphasized that there is a need to understand who the expert is, and what makes them an expert.

The major automakers are cognizant of this problem, and have been tackling these issues for some time. The new twist is not these problems themselves, but rather in articulating them through a reference frame of expert systems. It's a new way of seeing old ideas. With that in mind, let's now turn to how these companies are confronting these problems. We will dive into three key techniques being utilized in the self-driving car field, and discuss these techniques with reference to expert systems. The three key techniques are (1) Inverse Reinforcement Learning, (2) Generative Adversarial Networks or GAN, and (3) Dataset Aggregation or referred to as DAgger.

Let's start with Inverse Reinforcement Learning, and begin by discussing reinforcement learning overall and then bring the "inverse" aspect into the model. Reinforcement learning is a simple process to describe. You reward behaviors that best yield the desired outcome. You don't copy behaviors per se, instead you favor behaviors. This allows you to search for a most desired behavior over many iterations.

One straightforward example is merging lanes on the highway. If the merger is smooth, at a uniform speed, and no cars must suddenly shift out of the way, then one could consider this a desirable behavior. We can then create a cost function that articulates these parameters for the AI of the self-driving car and adjust probability weights in the model.

Unfortunately, while some algorithms make great use of this, such as Google's famous game playing system AlphaGo, for self-driving cars it is more complicated. Let's revisit the example of a car merging while on a highway. There is a myriad of behaviors that dictate a successful merger, and you cannot reasonably simplify it to just a handful of key elements. Accounting for and fine tuning these parameters is nearly impossible. This leads us to inverse reinforcement learning as another approach. We'll flip the model and use observed outputs to design our cost function.

We take a series of observed outputs, like successful lane mergers from human drivers, and have our model guess at a reward function. You then check this guessed model against the training instances. You might think this is a simple guess-and-check approach, but it's more complicated in many ways. We still provide it the optimal goal, and give it some key state identifiers. For a car merging, the goal might be to shift over X amount of feet, and the nearby identifiers might be road markers or adjacent cars. The rest is up to the machine to figure out, though it still "learns" through given algorithms (such as the max-margin based Discriminative Feature Learning which uses complex probability mapping to determine key features from sample data).

Let's briefly explore how this solves the two key problems earlier noted in expert systems. This circumvents the need for an expert by allowing us to use only successful attempts. While the issue of imperfect data still persists, it is mitigated since you don't have to select perfect data. As long as you provide successes exclusively, the car can level out the imperfections of each individual instance by observing all of the data. Thus, we don't need an expert, we simply need success. Does it matter who performed a surgery, if the surgery was successful? Perhaps it doesn't sit well to not know the nature of the expert, but to a machine seeking to produce optimum output it doesn't especially matter. We also avoid having to account for the human element, as the computer will intrinsically find features that allow it to mimic the process, performing better than a human in many cases.

Next, let's move onto our second key aspect in expert systems, the Generative Adversarial Network (GAN). Let's focus on the second word of that phrase, namely the word adversarial. The key idea of generative adversarial networks involves the use of two competing neural networks. Both learn on a set of training data. However, their roles differ. One attempts to create synthetic or so-called "fake" data, while the other attempts to discern between the generated fake data and real data. In this competitive environment, both networks are constantly getting better. One attempting to create more realistic data, the other attempting to get better at discerning between real and synthetic data. In this case, generative simply means to be continually generating the fake data.

Let's now look at some applications of this in self driving cars. One notable application is similar to inverse reinforcement learning, attempting to figure out what makes a human driver able to perform the driving task. We cannot necessarily tell what defines good driving, but perhaps we can discern what does not define good driving. This is where we can use GANs to our advantage. We use one network to create synthetic human driver data, while the other attempts to discern between real and fake data. This can allow us to hone our network onto which features best define a good driver. If you are having difficulty understanding how we can fake human data, just imagine a simple state transition matrix. The faking part would be the structure of the graph and the probabilities/rules associated with moving through the graph.

Another interesting example of GAN is for generating fully fake simulated environments with which to train models on. The objective is to create environments so close to reality that you can then generate all the data that you want for different self-driving car use cases. This is a relatively new idea, and came recently from Apple's SimGan, which utilizes simulated and unsupervised learning methods to generate excellent synthetic data. The beauty in this is the number of use cases. You can generate one round of synthetic data, and utilize it for any number of individual problems in the self-driving car domain, ranging from merging to accident avoidance. You can even generate different perspectives on the same state to try and further observe features.

Let's once again connect this into solving expert systems issues. Rather than focus on an expert themselves, we look primarily at the results of their work, and attempt to determine what is indicative of their work and what is not. We can use GANs to accomplish this goal.

Our last key technique is the Dataset Aggregation or DAgger algorithm. DAgger is a response to applying limited data to a new scenario. In many cases, this process is very difficult.

Suppose you had a race car that is being driven on a racetrack. Imagine you had a racetrack A where you had a single lap from an expert as training data. How could you apply this to a new racetrack B? With a lack of data, a neural network would have insufficient data to apply toward learning from it. In addition, if the neural network fails, it won't be able to locate a minimum error since almost every result ends in a failure state. This is a data mismatch issue. In terms of expert systems, the DAgger algorithm is tackling how we can take an expert with only a scarce amount of data from them, and apply the limited data to a new problem.

What DAgger does is aggregate data. It examines what the expert did and attempts to derive a policy from this. It then uses this policy to deterministically generate a new potential state for the next time it attempts a similar behavior. DAgger then adds these new potential states to its dataset, and considers this the new "expert," deciding the next state based upon the prior ones. This allows you to progressively build a dataset of inputs that the final policy is likely to encounter.

As an example, suppose you are attempting to teach a self-driving car how to make a right turn on a racetrack B and have setup a simulation to do so. You have the expert's data that was collected from racetrack A, so the computer has a limited sense of what a right turn is. At iteration one of the simulation, the car is not quite sure how much it should turn the steering wheel, so it fails to adequately steer the car and the car crashes into the left side wall. Quite unfortunate, but, the system had made a deterministic guess on what adjustments it should make to succeed in achieving the turn. Since it tried to make a right turn and failed, perhaps it might next guess that it should turn more to the right, and adds a series of such guesses to the progressively expanding "expert" dataset. With enough simulated iterations, it should end-up with a deep enough and finely tuned dataset to correctly make the right turn. In addition, it is better able to adapt to new situations based upon this collected dataset of learned experience.

Similar to the other two techniques, the Dagger algorithm is aiding in resolving the problems in developing expert systems for self-driving cars. You can see how this process mimics the trial-and-error that a normal expert would undergo. You make a mistake, and then you make a correction. This algorithm aids in building expert intuition into AI self-driving cars.

The aforementioned three techniques are ways to improve the capabilities of AI self-driving cars and do so via an augmented expert systems approach. It is an interesting way to understand the problems faced by the auto and tech industry in developing true self-driving cars, and indicates how computer science is advancing toward solving these problems.

APPENDIX

Dr. Lance Eliot and Michael B. Eliot

APPENDIX A
TEACHING WITH THIS MATERIAL

The material in this book can be readily used either as a supplemental to other content for a class, or it can also be used as a core set of textbook material for a specialized class. Classes where this material is most likely used include any classes at the college or university level that want to augment the class by offering thought provoking and educational essays about AI and self-driving cars.

In particular, here are some aspects for class use:

o   <u>Computer Science</u>. Studying AI, autonomous vehicles, etc.

o   <u>Business</u>. Exploring technology and it adoption for business.

o   <u>Sociology</u>. Sociological views on the adoption and advancement of technology.

Specialized classes at the undergraduate and graduate level can also make use of this material.

For each chapter, consider whether you think the chapter provides material relevant to your course topic. There is plenty of opportunity to get the students thinking about the topic and force them to decide whether they agree or disagree with the points offered and positions taken. I would also encourage you to have the students do additional research beyond the chapter material presented (I provide next some suggested assignments they can do).

RESEARCH ASSIGNMENTS ON THESE TOPICS

Your students can find background material on these topics, doing so in various business and technical publications. I list below the top ranked AI related journals. For business publications, I would suggest the usual culprits such as the Harvard Business Review, Forbes, Fortune, WSJ, and the like.

Here are some suggestions of homework or projects that you could assign to students:

a) <u>Assignment for foundational AI research topic</u>: Research and prepare a paper and a presentation on a specific aspect of Deep AI, Machine Learning, ANN, etc. The paper should cite at least 3 reputable sources. Compare and contrast to what has been stated in this book.

b) <u>Assignment for the Self-Driving Car topic</u>: Research and prepare a paper and Self-Driving Cars. Cite at least 3 reputable sources and analyze the characterizations. Compare and contrast to what has been stated in this book.

c) <u>Assignment for a Business topic</u>: Research and prepare a paper and a presentation on businesses and advanced technology. What is hot, and what is not? Cite at least 3 reputable sources. Compare and contrast to the depictions in this book.

d) <u>Assignment to do a Startup:</u> Have the students prepare a paper about how they might startup a business in this realm. They must submit a sound Business Plan for the startup. They could also be asked to present their Business Plan and so should also have a presentation deck to coincide with it.

You can certainly adjust the aforementioned assignments to fit to your particular needs and the class structure. You'll notice that I ask for 3 reputable cited sources for the paper writing based assignments. I usually steer students toward "reputable" publications, since otherwise they will cite some oddball source that has no credentials other than that they happened to write something and post it onto the Internet. You can define "reputable" in whatever way you prefer, for example some faculty think Wikipedia is not reputable while others believe it is reputable and allow students to cite it.

The reason that I usually ask for at least 3 citations is that if the student only does one or two citations they usually settle on whatever they happened to find the fastest. By requiring three citations, it usually seems to force them to look around, explore, and end-up probably finding five or more, and then whittling it down to 3 that they will actually use.

I have not specified the length of their papers, and leave that to you to tell the students what you prefer. For each of those assignments, you could end-up with a short one to two pager, or you could do a dissertation length paper. Base the length on whatever best fits for your class, and the credit amount of the assignment within the context of the other grading metrics you'll be using for the class.

I mention in the assignments that they are to do a paper and prepare a presentation. I usually try to get students to present their work. This is a good practice for what they will do in the business world. Most of the time, they will be required to prepare an analysis and present it. If you don't have the class time or inclination to have the students present, then you can of course cut out the aspect of them putting together a presentation.

If you want to point students toward highly ranked journals in AI, here's a list of the top journals as reported by *various citation counts sources* (this list changes year to year):

- o   Communications of the ACM
- o   Artificial Intelligence
- o   Cognitive Science
- o   IEEE Transactions on Pattern Analysis and Machine Intelligence
- o   Foundations and Trends in Machine Learning
- o   Journal of Memory and Language
- o   Cognitive Psychology
- o   Neural Networks
- o   IEEE Transactions on Neural Networks and Learning Systems
- o   IEEE Intelligent Systems
- o   Knowledge-based Systems

GUIDE TO USING THE CHAPTERS

For each of the chapters, I provide next some various ways to use the chapter material. You can assign the tasks as individual homework assignments, or the tasks can be used with team projects for the class. You can easily layout a series of assignments, such as indicating that the students are to do item "a" below for say Chapter 1, then "b" for the next chapter of the book, and so on.

a) What is the main point of the chapter and describe in your own words the significance of the topic,

b) Identify at least two aspects in the chapter that you agree with, and support your concurrence by providing at least one other outside researched item as support; make sure to explain your basis for disagreeing with the aspects,

c) Identify at least two aspects in the chapter that you disagree with, and support your disagreement by providing at least one other outside researched item as support; make sure to explain your basis for disagreeing with the aspects,

d) Find an aspect that was not covered in the chapter, doing so by conducting outside research, and then explain how that aspect ties into the chapter and what significance it brings to the topic,

e) Interview a specialist in industry about the topic of the chapter, collect from them their thoughts and opinions, and readdress the chapter by citing your source and how they compared and contrasted to the material,

f) Interview a relevant academic professor or researcher in a college or university about the topic of the chapter, collect from them their thoughts and opinions, and readdress the chapter by citing your source and how they compared and contrasted to the material,

g) Try to update a chapter by finding out the latest on the topic, and ascertain whether the issue or topic has now been solved or whether it is still being addressed, explain what you come up with.

The above are all ways in which you can get the students of your class involved in considering the material of a given chapter. You could mix things up by having one of those above assignments per each week, covering the chapters over the course of the semester or quarter.

As a reminder, here are the chapters of the book and you can select whichever chapters you find most valued for your particular class:

Companion Book By This Author

Advances in AI and Autonomous Vehicles: Cybernetic Self-Driving Cars

Practical Advances in Artificial Intelligence (AI) and Machine Learning

by

Dr. Lance B. Eliot, MBA, PhD

Chapter Title

This title is available via Amazon and other book sellers

Companion Book By This Author
Self-Driving Cars:
"The Mother of All AI Projects"
by Dr. Lance B. Eliot, MBA, PhD

This title is available via Amazon and other book sellers

Companion Book By This Author

Innovation and Thought Leadership on Self-Driving Driverless Cars

by Dr. Lance B. Eliot, MBA, PhD

This title is available via Amazon and other book sellers

Dr. Lance Eliot and Michael B. Eliot

Companion Book By This Author

New Advances in AI Autonomous Driverless Cars Self-Driving Cars

by Dr. Lance B. Eliot, MBA, PhD

This title is available via Amazon and other book sellers

ADDENDUM

Autonomous Vehicle Driverless Self-Driving Cars and Artificial Intelligence

Practical Advances in Artificial Intelligence (AI) and Machine Learning

By
Dr. Lance Eliot and Michael B. Eliot

————

For supplemental materials of this book, visit:
www.lance-blog.com

For special orders of this book, contact:
LBE Press Publishing
Email: LBE.Press.Publishing@gmail.com

ABOUT THE AUTHORS

Dr. Lance Eliot, MBA, PhD is the CEO of Techbruim, Inc. and Executive Director of the Cybernetic Self-Driving Car Institute, and has over twenty years of industry experience including serving as a corporate officer in a billion dollar firm and was a partner in a major executive services firm. He is also a serial entrepreneur having founded, ran, and sold several high-tech related businesses. He previously hosted the popular radio show *Technotrends* that was also available on American Airlines flights via their in-flight audio program. Author or co-author of over a dozen books and more than 400 articles, he has made appearances on CNN, and has been a frequent speaker at industry conferences.

A former professor at the University of Southern California (USC), he founded and led an innovative research lab on Artificial Intelligence in Business. Known as the "AI Insider" his writings on AI advances and trends has been widely read and cited. He also previously served on the faculty of the University of California Los Angeles (UCLA), and was a visiting professor at other major universities. He was elected to the International Board of the Society for Information Management (SIM), a prestigious association of over 3,000 high-tech executives worldwide. Dr. Eliot holds a PhD from USC, MBA, and Bachelor's in Computer Science, and earned the CDP, CCP, CSP, CDE, and CISA certifications. .

Michael B. Eliot is an entrepreneur and currently nearing completion of his Bachelor's degree in Computer Science at the University of California Berkeley, one of the topmost ranked computer science programs in the world. His work experience includes serving as a software engineer at an upcoming self-driving car company (Tesloop, Inc.), he served as a software engineer at Activision Blizzard, Inc., and he's been a research systems engineer at the innovative Autonomous Drone Lab at UC Berkeley.

In addition, he has competed successfully in several prominent hackathons including the Yale Hackathon, and has received awards and accolades for his efforts. He has written for the Berkeley Technology Review (BTR), interned for the Vice Chair of the Congressional Committee on Science & Technology, and been an invited presenter of his original research at the Lawrence Livermore National Laboratory (LLNL) and at the American Association for the Advancement of Science (AAAS) annual conference. He has extensively traveled and was an entrepreneur-in-residence for the European EIA high-tech entrepreneurship program in France.